Unleash The Celebration

10 Graduation Party Ideas That Will Leave You Speechless

Eric Bob

Unleash The Celebration

10 Graduation Party Ideas That
Will Leave You Speechless

this material, including mistakes, omissions, or inaccuracies.

Table Of Content

Introduction 6

Chapter 1 9

Congratulations On Accomplishing This Significant Milestone! 9

Chapter 2 20

The Value of A Remarkable Graduation Party 20

Chapter 3 42

Theme Selection: Creating an Unforgettable Party 42

Chapter 4 62

Party Planning Requirements 62

Chapter 5 90

Ideas for Graduation Parties That Will Leave You Speechless 90

Chapter 6 154

Success Planning 154

Chapter 7 169

Graduation Party Planning Tips 169

Chapter 8 190

Etiquette for Graduation Parties 190

Conclusion 206

Introduction

"Unleash the Celebration: 10 Graduation Party Ideas That Will Leave You Speechless" welcomes you! Graduation is a significant event that marks the culmination of years of great work, commitment, and progress. It's time to celebrate accomplishments, say goodbye to an unforgettable chapter, and look forward to the exciting opportunities that await. And what better way you can commemorate this occasion than holding a speechless graduation party?

In this e-book, we've compiled a list of 10 incredible graduation party ideas that will turn your celebration into an unforgettable event. Your guests will be taken into a world of magic, excitement, and pure joy the moment they enter the site. Each concept has been thoughtfully developed to pique your interest, fire your creativity, and assist you in planning a graduation celebration that will be remembered for years.

Prepare to enter a world of great possibilities as we lead you through various intriguing and distinctive topics. We offer the right inspiration to complement your style, whether you anticipate an outdoor spectacular surrounded by nature's splendor or an elegant gala exuding refinement. Want to send your visitors back in time with a throwback blast from the past or take them on an unforgettable travel adventure? There is no need for yu to look any further. We have ideas for every taste, ensuring your graduation celebration accurately represents your personality and achievements.

But it does not end there. This e-book is jam-packed with valuable ideas and insider information to help you arrange your event with simplicity and finesse. We can help you with anything from finance and guest list management to venue selection and invitation etiquette. We will give you a complete party planning roadmap, including a timetable and checklist, to ensure every aspect is remembered.

"Unleash the Celebration: 10 Graduation Party Ideas That Will Leave You Speechless" is the definitive guide to making a fantastic event, whether you're a graduate organizing your party or a loved one trying to make a memorable celebration. Prepare to go on a journey of inspiration, creativity, and celebration as we reveal the secrets of throwing an unforgettable graduation party.

Are you ready to let loose and throw a graduation party that will leave everyone speechless? Let's plunge in together and explore the astounding possibilities!

Chapter 1

Congratulations On Accomplishing This Significant Milestone!

Congratulations on accomplishing this significant milestone! Whether you are a student who has recently completed your academic journey or a happy parent, family member, or friend, this occasion should be honored. You've put in many hours of hard work, devotion, and drive to get here, and it's time to recognize and respect your accomplishments.

Graduation is an important life event. It results from years of study, progress, and personal development. From the very first day in school to the last, you've been on a journey full of obstacles, accomplishments, and invaluable experiences. You've overcome challenges, broadened your knowledge, and discovered new interests. Now that you're on the verge of a new chapter, it's time to take stock of everything you've done.

This moment is about more than simply the diplomas and degrees you've received; it's about the lessons you've learned, the friendships you've formed, and the memories you've made. It is about the personal growth and transformation you have through. Graduation demonstrates your tenacity, persistence, and dedication to greatness. It represents your willingness to take on new challenges and seize new chances.

Remember the late-night study sessions, the moments of self-doubt, and the sacrifices you took to get to this point as you reflect on your journey. Consider the mentors, professors, and loved ones who have helped you along the path. Graduation is more than simply your accomplishment; it is a group success shared by those who have supported, encouraged, and believed in you. Acknowledge the people who also have helped you along your educational path for their counsel and continuous support.

This landmark is more than simply the destination; it is also about the trip. The difficulties you encountered, the skills you learned, and the information you obtained prepared you for the future. Graduation serves as a springboard for fresh beginnings and opportunities. It's time to create objectives, follow your aspirations, and make a difference. Whether entering further education, the workforce, or starting a personal adventure, remember that the skills and lessons you've gained will be essential assets in molding your future.

As you prepare to celebrate your graduation, reflect on your achievements. Recognize your accomplishments in terms of personal development and progress. Celebrate the relationships that have grown and the memories that have been made. Your graduation party is more than simply a get-together; it's a sign of victory, an occasion to recognize your journey and the individuals who have been a part of it.

Accept this celebration with enthusiasm, excitement, and pride. Allow it to remind you of your tenacity, persistence, and capacity to overcome obstacles. Your graduation party is a unique opportunity to celebrate in a style that correctly shows your personality and accomplishments.

Remember, as you start on the next chapter of your life, this mark the beginning. Your graduation is a stepping stone to a lifetime of development and discovery, not the conclusion of your learning journey. Accept new possibilities, be open to new experiences, and continue to seek knowledge and personal development.

Congratulations on attaining this significant milestone once more. Your tenacity, devotion, and hard work have paid off. It is time to rejoice, preserve the memories, and look forward to a shining and hopeful future. This is your time to glow, and we are here to rejoice with you as you unleash the party and make your graduation one to remember.

A Summary of The Significance of Graduation Parties

Graduation celebrations have a particular place in our hearts since they symbolize the end of an important chapter in our lives. They are more than simply social events; they serve as a symbolic link among the past and the future, a time to recognize accomplishments, and a chance to celebrate personal progress and success. These gatherings are significant for graduates and their loved ones, as they create memories that will last a lifetime.

One of the primary reasons that graduation celebrations are so important is that they allow graduates to acknowledge and celebrate their hard work, commitment, and tenacity throughout their educational journey. A graduation is a significant event that marks the successful conclusion of a level of education, whether it be high school, college, or postgraduate study. It culminates years of academic efforts, late-night study sessions, complex tests, and knowledge and skill growth.

Graduation celebrations are about recognizing personal development and transformation in addition to academic achievement. They reflect a period of self-discovery when people had the chance to explore their interests, develop their abilities, and grow. Graduates have obtained knowledge in their study subjects and vital life skills such as critical thinking, problem-solving, collaboration, and resilience. A graduation celebration recognizes and respects this complete development, recognizing the well-rounded individuals ready to embark on the next chapter of their life.

Furthermore, graduation celebrations provide an opportunity for introspection and thankfulness. They allow graduates to show gratitude to family members, friends, instructors, and mentors who have supported and mentored them along the journey. These gatherings provide opportunities for graduates to express their genuine thanks to those who have played a key role in their educational path. It's time to express gratitude for the consistent support, encouragement, and faith in their skills.

Graduation celebrations are essential for more than just personal reasons. They bring together a community of loved ones, friends, and well-wishers who have played a role in the graduates' lives. As individuals meet to celebrate a shared accomplishment, these events promote a sense of belonging and create long-lasting ties. Graduation celebrations frequently bring together friends who may have drifted apart after high school or college, allowing them to reminisce, strengthen friendships, and enjoy their experiences together.

Graduation celebrations also function as a rite of passage, commemorating the movement from one stage of life to the next. They signify a point of completion, allowing graduates to say goodbye to established routines, habits, and surroundings and embrace the unknown possibilities that lay ahead. Graduation celebrations represent the start of new adventures, whether furthering one's education, entering the workforce, or pursuing personal goals. These festivities are an emotional bridge, allowing graduates to progress with a sense of success, confidence, and joy.

Finally, graduation parties are simply occasions for celebration and enjoyment! They are cheerful and celebratory celebrations filled with laughter, happiness, and accomplishment. It's a chance for graduates to unwind, relax, and spend time with their loved ones. Graduation celebrations frequently include engaging activities, excellent food, and vibrant entertainment, all contributing to a joyful atmosphere reflecting the spirit of achievement and celebration.

Finally, graduation celebrations are significant in our life. They are more than just gatherings; they are tremendous occasions to recognize accomplishments, celebrate personal progress, and welcome a new stage of life. These gatherings unite people, create lasting memories, and allow individuals to show their thanks. They remind the graduates of their hard work, effort, and devotion throughout their educational journey. So, let the party begin and make memories that will last a lifetime.

The e-Book's Purpose And What Readers Should Expect

"Unleash the Celebration: 10 Graduation Party Ideas That Will Leave You Speechless" is our new e-book! We want to present you with a wealth of inspiration, innovative ideas, and practical recommendations in this exciting guide to help you arrange a graduation celebration that will exceed all expectations. Whether you're a graduate seeking to celebrate your achievements or a loved one trying to plan a special celebration, this e-book is your go-to guide.

This e-book aims to help you unlock your ideas and kindle your creativity when preparing for a graduation celebration. We recognize that this is a massive milestone in your life, and we want to ensure that your celebration matches the significance of your accomplishments. We've hand-picked ten graduation party ideas that are one-of-a-kind, intriguing, and sure to leave you and your guests breathless.

You can anticipate thoroughly examining many party themes in this e-book, ranging from the charming to the glamorous, from the whimsical to the daring. We encourage you to go outside the box and plan a party that reflects your individuality and flair. We have the right concept to make your party memorable, whether you're planning an outdoor fiesta beneath the stars or a retro-inspired blast from the past.

But we continue beyond just giving you theme suggestions. We go into each notion in-depth, providing practical solutions for bringing your selected theme to life. We provide imaginative and new solutions to make every element of your celebration unforgettable, from décor and lighting to food and beverages. Every aspect, from the invites to the entertainment, should contribute to an immersive and unique experience for you and your guests.

In addition to theme-specific ideas, we offer basic suggestions and recommendations for organizing and executing a grand graduation celebration. Budgeting, guest list management, venue selection, and invitation etiquette are all covered. We provide a detailed calendar and checklist to assist you in staying organized and ensuring that every item is addressed. We aim to provide you with the knowledge and resources to arrange your party quickly.

We look at the emotional value of a graduation celebration and the practical ones. We recognize that this celebration is about more than simply décor and entertainment; it's about acknowledging your accomplishments, thanking those who have helped you, and enjoying the move into a new period of life. We discuss graduation party etiquette, gift-giving requirements, and how to make your visitors feel welcomed and respected. We want your party to be more than a gathering; we want it to be a passionate and meaningful celebration of your achievements.

Prepare to be inspired, encouraged, and excited for your graduation celebration as you read this e-book. We invite you to go beyond the box, let your imagination run wild, and make your celebration reflect your path and goals. We present real-life samples, breathtaking pictures, and anecdotes of significant events to spark your imagination and fuel your planning process.

Finally, this e-book aims to provide you with the tools you need to throw a graduation celebration that surpasses your expectations and impacts everyone who attends. We want to help you celebrate your achievements, remember the memories you've made, and look forward to the exciting opportunities that await you. We want your graduation celebration to be something you and your guests remember for years.

So, prepare to let lose the party! Allow this e-book to guide you as you begin arranging an unforgettable graduation celebration. Accept the ideas, the process, and, most importantly, the joy and excitement of celebrating your accomplishments. At every step of the journey, we are here to inspire, encourage, and celebrate with you.

Chapter 2

The Value of A Remarkable Graduation Party

Graduation is an important life event representing the culmination of years of hard work, devotion, and personal development. It's a significant occasion that needs to be remembered and honored meaningfully. A graduation party is ideal for appreciating and commemorating this considerable achievement. It is more than simply a party; it produces enduring memories and has a particular place in the hearts of graduates and their loved ones. Let's examine the significance of a memorable graduation celebration and why it's worth your time, effort, and ingenuity.

A spectacular graduation party, first and foremost, is a reflection and celebration of the graduate's accomplishments. It recognizes their tenacity, dedication, and academic achievements. It's a time to reflect on the struggles conquered, the sacrifices made, and the personal progress gained over the educational journey. A well-planned and well-performed graduation celebration demonstrates the graduate's hard work and devotion, instilling pride and affirmation. It's an opportunity to recognize their accomplishments meaningfully and meaningfully.

A spectacular graduation celebration also serves as an opportunity to express thanks and appreciation. Graduates are not alone in reaching this milestone; they have a network of family, friends, and mentors who have encouraged and mentored them along the journey. The reception serves as a forum for thanking these essential persons, recognizing their accomplishments, and celebrating the joint efforts that enabled the graduate's achievement. It builds appreciation, improves connections, and generates treasured memories of love and support.

A memorable graduation celebration also serves as a link between the past and the future. It's time to say goodbye to the educational journey's familiar routines, friendships, and experiences and embrace the thrilling opportunities that await. The party acts as a symbolic shift, allowing graduates to reflect on their progress, lessons gained, and future goals. It's an opportunity to honor previous successes and the hopes and dreams determining the graduate's future path. A well-planned graduation celebration instills enthusiasm, motivation, and eagerness for the next chapter of life.

A wonderful graduation celebration draws people together as well. It is a gathering of friends, classmates, and family members who have shared the graduate's journey. It fosters a sense of excitement, laughter, and camaraderie as loved ones gather to celebrate a shared accomplishment. The celebration is transformed into a venue for reuniting, remembering, and building friendships. It's a chance to make new memories and build ties, providing a sense of community and support as graduates go on to their next life stage.

A wonderful graduation celebration provides an opportunity to display creativity, personality, and personal relevance. It allows the graduate to exhibit their distinct character, interests, and style. The party theme, décor, and activities may all be customized to match the graduate's interests, accomplishments, or future goals. It's an opportunity to create an immersive and customized experience that will leave guests with a lasting impression. A well-planned graduation celebration reflects the graduate's identity and acts as a monument to their uniqueness.

Finally, a memorable graduation celebration is an inspiration and motivational source for future generations. When graduates and their guests see how much work goes into preparing and executing a spectacular celebration, it establishes a precedent for future accomplishments. It inspires people to have high dreams, work hard, and strive for perfection. A spectacular graduation party serves as an inspiration not only for the graduate but also for all those who attend and watch the event.

Finally, a memorable graduation celebration is essential in the lives of graduates and their loved ones. It is a moment to recognize accomplishments, express appreciation, celebrate personal progress, and anticipate the future. A spectacular graduation party is more than just a gathering; it is a treasured memory, a mark of success, and a source of encouragement. It fosters a sense of joy, solidarity, and gratitude. So, put in the time, effort, and ingenuity necessary to organize a graduation celebration that will be remembered for years. Allow it to reflect your journey, celebrate your accomplishments, and be a tribute to the bright future ahead.

The Importance of Graduation Parties

Graduation celebrations are essential. They are more than just social gatherings or calendar events. They are significant and hold a variety of meanings for graduates, their families, and their communities. These events highlight the culmination of years of dedication, persistence, and personal development. They provide an opportunity to recognize accomplishments, express thanks, and welcome the move into a new stage of life. Let's examine why graduation celebrations are essential and why they have a particular place in our hearts.

First and foremost, graduation celebrations are essential because they honor and celebrate students' academic achievements. Graduation from high school, college, or postgraduate study represents the successful conclusion of a substantial educational journey. It reflects the accumulation of information, abilities, and experiences that will affect the future pursuits of graduates. A graduation celebration is an opportunity to recognize and enjoy the hard work, commitment, and sacrifices that have led to this achievement. It allows graduates to revel in their achievements' excitement and satisfaction, knowing they are being recognized and honored.

Furthermore, graduation celebrations are essential because they allow relatives and loved ones to gather together and express their support for the graduate. Every successful graduate is supported by a network of family members, friends, and mentors who offer advice, encouragement, and steadfast support throughout their education. These gatherings allow loved ones to show delight, excitement, and appreciation for the graduate's accomplishments. It's a time to express "we are proud of you" and show the collective love and support that has enabled the graduate to attain this momentous milestone.

Graduation celebrations are essential beyond the individual level because they build a feeling of community and shared success. They bring together classmates, friends, and community members who have shared the graduate's journey. These events provide a collaborative celebration in which everyone may partake in the graduates' accomplishments and milestones. They serve as a reminder that education is a collaborative endeavor, and one person's success benefits the entire community. Graduation parties become occasions for individuals from all walks of life to celebrate and encourage one another.

Graduation celebrations are also important because they create a feeling of closure and transition. Graduation signals the conclusion of one stage of life and the start of another. It's time to bid farewell to old habits, classes, and friendships. Graduation celebrations provide a point of reflection for graduates, allowing them to reflect on the memories, experiences, and lessons learned during their educational journey. They allow graduates to show their thanks to instructors, mentors, and friends who have significantly impacted their lives. Simultaneously, these events provide a forum for embracing the unknown possibilities and chances that lie ahead. They serve as a symbolic bridge, assisting graduates in moving forward with a sense of closure, gratitude, and joy.

Graduation celebrations are significant because they produce lasting memories and joyful moments. These occasions are filled with joy, laughter, and a sense of success. They allow graduates to unwind, have fun, and enjoy the company of their loved ones. Graduation celebrations frequently include exciting activities, music, and delectable cuisine, all contributing to a joyous mood. These moments of delight and celebration become treasured memories that graduates and their loved ones may reflect on with affection and nostalgia.

Finally, graduation celebrations are significant because they encourage and motivate future generations. Young students are inspired to dream large and strive for excellence when they see graduates' joys and accomplishments. Graduation celebrations become emblems of possibility, encouraging young minds that they, too, can achieve their objectives and celebrate their achievements with hard work, commitment, and support. These events inspire future graduates, encouraging them to persist in the face of adversity and achieve their aspirations.

Graduation celebrations are important because they recognize achievements, unite communities, give closure and transition, create lasting memories, and inspire future generations. They are manifestations of hard effort, devotion, and personal development. So, let us embrace the significance of graduation celebrations and celebrate these landmarks with pleasure, gratitude, and a profound appreciation for education's transformational potential.

Leaving A Lasting Impression On The Graduate and Guests

Creating lasting memories is essential to every noteworthy occasion, including graduation celebrations. These events signify a crucial milestone in the life of a graduate, representing years of hard work, progress, and success. By planning a memorable graduation party, you may ensure that the graduate and their guests will remember the occasion for years. Let's look at ways to make long-lasting memories that will have an influence.

Creating a welcoming and joyous atmosphere is one of the most critical aspects of creating memorable memories. Visitors should be filled with excitement and expectation when they arrive at the graduation celebration. Consider including unique elements that represent the graduate's personality, such as a picture wall with memorable events from their educational path or a display of their achievements. Set the tone with vivid décor, upbeat music, and a welcoming atmosphere that inspires visitors to unwind, connect, and celebrate.

Interactive activities and entertainment can also create long-lasting memories. Consider including items that will engage guests and urge them to participate. Photo booths with props and backgrounds are usually popular because they give visitors a fun and hiring opportunity to record memories together. You may also incorporate games or tournaments that bring together people of all ages, encouraging laughter, friendly competition, and shared experiences. These games not only help to create memories, but they also work as icebreakers, encouraging visitors to mingle and form new relationships.

Furthermore, including personal touches in the graduation celebration may significantly improve the experience. When arranging the event, take the time to consider the graduate's passions, hobbies, and interests. Add parts of the graduate's special gift or skill, such as music, art, or athletics, to the celebration. For example, if the graduate is musically inclined, build a spot for live performances or a playlist of their favorite tunes.

Make the occasion more memorable and essential by customizing it.

Heartfelt speeches or messages are another effective technique to leave a lasting impression. Allow family, friends, and mentors to offer their views and convey their happiness and appreciation for the graduate. These meaningful remarks leave a lasting impression on the graduate's heart and create memories that will be treasured for years. Consider scheduling speeches throughout the reception or presenting a guestbook where visitors may leave their good wishes and words of wisdom. These gestures celebrate the graduation while creating a sense of connection and community among the visitors.

The importance of images in preserving memories cannot be emphasized. Encourage attendees to take photos of memorable moments during the party by giving disposable cameras, setting up a designated photo location, or developing a hashtag for visitors to use when sharing their photos on social media. Consider hiring a professional photographer to capture the occasion as well. These images, which capture the celebration's pleasure, love, and excitement, will be treasured souvenirs for the graduate. They will elicit recollections and feelings, allowing the graduate and their loved ones to relive the memorable occasion long after it has passed.

Food and beverages can also help to create long-lasting memories. Consider including special meals or sweets that are meaningful to the graduate. It might be their favorite comfort meal, a family recipe, or a dish from their ancestry. By providing a range of alternatives, including vegetarian and allergy-friendly meals, all visitors will feel included and cared for. Consider designing a distinctive drink or cocktail representing the graduation party's theme or spirit. These smart culinary choices will not only please visitors' taste senses but also provide a memorable touch to the occasion.

Finally, delivering meaningful and unique party goodies may impact your attendees. Consider choosing favors corresponding to the graduate's hobbies or the party's theme. Personalized products like keychains, magnets, or engraved bookmarks can serve as long-lasting souvenirs of the occasion.

First and foremost, creating a pleasant and appealing atmosphere is essential for setting the tone for the celebration. Take into account the location, layout, lighting, and decorations. Choose an area that can adequately accommodate your guests and fits the intended ambiance of the event. Please ensure the place is clean, well-organized, and aesthetically attractive, whether it's an outside garden, a hired event venue, or the comfort of your home.

Lighting is essential in setting the perfect tone for the celebration. Dim, soft lighting may create an intimate and comforting feeling, but brighter lighting can stimulate and inspire a dynamic mood. To emphasize essential locations or decorations, consider combining ambient lightings, such as string lights or candles, with targeted lighting, such as spotlights or uplighting. Experiment with various lighting approaches to get the appropriate ambiance that corresponds to the celebration's theme.

Following that, picking an engaging theme may add excitement and cohesion to the party. An article might be inspired by the graduate's interests, future goals, or a unique notion that fits their personality. For example, if the graduate is a travel enthusiast, you might construct a "Wanderlust Adventure" theme with globes, maps, and travel-inspired décor. A well-executed piece may drive the selection of décor, activities, and even the meal, providing visitors with a unified and immersive experience.

Once you've decided on a theme, it's time to focus on the finer elements of the decorations. Consider including customized aspects representing the graduate's path, accomplishments, or hobbies. A picture wall displaying memorable occasions, trophies, and diplomas or a timeline highlighting the graduate's educational progress might all be included. These customized touches provide aesthetic flair and act as conversation starters and reminders of the graduate's achievements.

Another critical part of planning a grand celebration is maintaining a seamless and well-planned flow of events. Consider the party's timetable and the order of events. Make a timetable that permits visitors to participate in various activities during the celebration. You may begin with a welcome reception and a short statement or toast to celebrate the graduation. Then, integrate interactive activities or entertainment to keep guests involved and entertained. Allow for breaks, chats, and transitions between different celebration elements by keeping the party rhythm in mind.

Food and drinks are necessary components of every successful gathering. When arranging the food, keep your guests' tastes and dietary limitations in mind. Provide a range of selections to suit varied preferences, such as vegetarian, vegan, and gluten-free options. You can choose a buffet, a sit-down meal, or even a specialized food station, depending on the nature of the event. As the culinary experience plays a crucial part in visitor happiness and enjoyment, ensure that the presentation and food are appealing.

Activities and entertainment are essential components of a successful celebration. Consider including interactive features that will engage guests and provide unforgettable experiences. Hiring a DJ or live band to offer music and entertainment, creating games or competitions to encourage guest engagement, or even arranging for a surprise performance that corresponds with the party's theme are all options. These activities energize the celebration, develop connections among attendees, and make a lasting impact on those who attend.

Finally, communication and organization are essential for a successful celebration. Inform your attendees about the event's specifics, including the date, time, venue, and special instructions or requests. Use digital invites or social media event sites to keep everyone informed and create a forum for attendees to communicate and ask questions. Create a checklist or a timetable to keep track of duties and verify that everything is ready for the celebration.

In conclusion, creating a welcoming ambiance, selecting a captivating theme, paying attention to details, planning a well-paced flow of events, offering delicious food and beverages, incorporating interactive activities, and ensuring effective communication and organization all contribute to a successful celebration. By considering these characteristics, you can design an atmosphere that engages guests, depicts the graduate's journey, and leaves an impression on everyone in attendance. So, invest your creativity and effort into creating a memorable and outstanding graduation party that will be remembered fondly for years to come.

Ideas for Graduation Outfits

Your graduation day is an important occasion that necessitates stunning clothes befitting the occasion. It's perfect for displaying your unique style, displaying confidence, and making a long-lasting fashion statement. We have some great graduation dress ideas to inspire you, whether you like a classic and elegant look or want to express yourself with a one-of-a-kind combination.

1. Timeless Elegance: Choose a fitted dress or a sleek pantsuit for a traditional and timeless style.

Accessorize with delicate jewelry and a structured purse in a neutral color palette such as black, navy, or white. This refined combination will have you feeling poised, polished, and available to take on the world.

2. flower Fantasy: Celebrate nature's beauty with a gorgeous floral dress or romper. Pick a print that expresses your personality, whether gentle and feminine or solid and bright. Finish the ensemble with wedges, heels, and minimal accessories to let the flowery design shine. This attire exudes happiness and celebrates the beginning of a new season in your life.

3. Playful Jumpsuit: A fashionable jumpsuit can make a fashion-forward statement. Choose a fitted silhouette in a bright color or a stylish pattern. Pair it with dramatic accessories like a broad belt or a spectacular necklace to add a touch of glam. A jumpsuit oozes confidence and highlights your sense of style, making it an ideal choice for a modern and fashionable graduation appearance.

4. Feminine Fashion: Wear a flowing maxi dress or a midi skirt with a shirt to embrace your

femininity. Choose soft pastel colors or romantic patterns to get a whimsical and ethereal vibe. Accessorize with delicate jewelry and elegant sandals or ballet flats. As you stroll, this combination will make you feel beautiful and effortlessly elegant.

5. Dapper and Sharp: Consider a fitted jacket with tailored slacks or a sleek jumpsuit for a more masculine-inspired outfit. Choose a monochrome or neutral color palette with a bright tie or pocket square to provide a flash of color. Complete the look with polished dress shoes and a tidy hairdo. This outfit oozes confidence and highlights your exquisite sense of taste.

6. Statement outfit: Make a dramatic statement with an attention-grabbing outfit. Choose a dress that reflects your personality, whether a brilliant color, rich detailing, or a distinctive silhouette. Allow the dress to take center stage by pairing it with matching accessories. This look will have you feeling like a true fashion icon, ready to turn heads and leave an everlasting impression.

7. Chic and Casual: Choose a chic and casual combination for a more relaxed and comfortable

look. High-waisted jeans or pants look great with a fashionable shirt or fitted jacket. Finish the appearance with attractive sneakers or ankle boots for a stylish touch. This costume blends comfort and style, allowing you to celebrate casually yet stylishly.

Remember that staying true to yourself and embracing your particular style is the key to finding the proper graduation attire. Choose an outfit that lets you feel confident and comfortable, as well as one that reflects your personality. Let your dress celebrate your accomplishments and the exciting path ahead, whether you choose timeless elegance, colorful patterns, or fashion-forward pieces.

As you go across the stage to get your graduation, remember that you display your academic achievements and pure elegance. Embrace this historical event, exude confidence, and let your graduation attire represent the extraordinary person you have become.

Congratulations, graduate, and may your graduation attire reflect your unique personality and testimony to your incredible journey!

Chapter 3

Theme Selection: Creating an Unforgettable Party

One of the most essential steps in arranging a memorable party is deciding on the ideal theme. The theme establishes the tone for the whole event, resulting in an immersive and seamless experience for both the host and the attendees. A well-chosen piece can transform an average party into something exceptional, creating a lasting impact on everyone in attendance. Let's look at the significance of these choices and how they may set the tone for a memorable party.

First and foremost, a well-chosen theme contributes to creating a unified and visually appealing ambiance. It gives a framework for choosing decorations, colors, and dresses, ensuring that every celebration aspect is consistent with the theme. A coherent article links all the components together, producing a harmonic and aesthetically attractive atmosphere, whether it's a fanciful fairy tale theme, a glamorous Hollywood soirée, or a colorful tropical paradise. Guests will be quickly transported into an immersive and one-of-a-kind experience, setting the stage for an unforgettable celebration.

Furthermore, a theme adds excitement and anticipation to the event. When attendees get an invitation or learn about the chosen theme, it piques their interest and builds tension. A well-executed piece piques attendees' interest and motivates them to interact and engage with the party on a deeper level. They may anxiously arrange their attire, devise inventive ways to incorporate the theme, or even make themed gifts or surprises for the host. The enthusiasm and anticipation around the theme add to the overall energy and mood of the party, making it a genuinely unforgettable event.

A well-chosen theme may lead to choices of entertainment and activities and create an aesthetically attractive ambiance. It offers a foundation for creating interactive experiences that captivate guests and leave them with lasting impressions. If the theme is a masquerade ball, visitors can participate in a mask-making class or enjoy a bustling dance floor with a professional ballroom dancer. Visitors can compete in sandcastle construction or watch a limbo contest if the theme is a beach party. The piece is the spark for one-of-a-kind and exciting activities that complement the overall idea, keeping visitors interested and engaged throughout the event.

A well-chosen theme also gives a personal and meaningful touch to the gathering. The article might represent the host's or guest of honor's interests, hobbies, or passions, making it a unique party. A sports-themed party might include items from their favorite team or sport if the graduate is a big sports lover. A Great Gatsby-inspired theme might take guests to the glittering world of the Roaring Twenties if the host is enthusiastic about a specific era, such as the 1920s. By incorporating personal touches into the theme, the party reflects the host's personality and fosters a stronger bond between the visitors and the occasion.

A well-chosen topic can also spark conversations and friendships among guests. It acts as a connecting thread, bringing individuals together and providing possibilities for connection and participation. Whether discussing their favorite characters, swapping costume ideas, or reminiscing about relevant experiences, guests may bond via their familiar excitement for the subject. A theme serves as an icebreaker, encouraging interactions and creating a feeling of community among visitors who may not have known one another before the party. The article motivates mingling, networking, and making new contacts, enhancing the entire party experience.

A theme may spark creativity and urge people to move beyond their comfort zones. It serves as a platform for self-expression and encourages people to use their imagination. A theme enables visitors to think outside the box and interact in a playful and inventive manner, whether via costume choices, related activities, or unique décor. It becomes a vehicle for self-expression, allowing guests to channel their inner kid and revel in the delight and excitement of adopting the theme. This creative environment lends a sense of joy and spontaneity to the party, making it stand out as a one-of-a-kind and unforgettable event.

Finally, theme selection is critical in creating the tone for a fantastic celebration. A well-chosen theme creates a visually appealing ambiance, builds excitement and anticipation, informs the choice of activities and entertainment, adds a personal and meaningful touch, sparks dialogues and relationships among attendees, and stimulates creativity. You can create a genuinely immersive and lasting experience for everyone in attendance by picking a theme that connects with the host or guest of honor and matches the party's overall objective. So, let your creativity go wild and embrace the power of theme choices to throw a party that your guests will remember for years to come.

Investigating Various Theme Possibilities

Exploring several theme alternatives while arranging a memorable party can be an exciting and creative process. The theme establishes the tone for the whole event and contributes to a seamless and immersive experience for both the host and the visitors. Several possibilities range from fanciful and magical themes to beautiful and refined thoughts. Let's explore themes to find enticing options for taking your party to the next level.

1. Enchanted Garden: You may transform your party site into a beautiful paradise with an Enchanted Garden theme. Use lush foliage, glittering fairy lights, and flower accents to create a fanciful and ethereal environment. Guests are encouraged to wear flower crowns, flowing gowns, or fairy-inspired clothes. DIY terrarium classes, flower arranging stations, and even a mystical treasure hunt are possible activities.

2. Casino Royale: A Casino Royale theme will bring the splendor and excitement of a high-end casino to your celebration. Set up blackjack, poker, and roulette tables, and supply guests with play money for a fantastic gambling experience. Decorate the space with glittering decorations, rich velvet curtains, and flashing lighting.

Encourage attendees to dress formally and provide specialty drinks and hors d'oeuvres.

3. Vintage Carnival: A Vintage Carnival-themed celebration emanates nostalgia and old-world charm. You can create a vivid and playful mood with striped tents, carnival games, and bright balloons. Classic carnival delicacies such as popcorn, cotton candy, and hot dogs are available to guests. Include live entertainment like jugglers, stilt walkers, and a vintage photo booth to let guests remember the joyous day.

4. Starry Night: A Starry Night theme will transport your guests to a fantastic dimension. String lights, luminous stars, and heavenly components can be used to decorate the venue. Make a comfortable lounge area with floor pillows and luxurious blankets for guests to rest and gaze at the "stars." Serve celestial-inspired beverages and pastries, and think about hiring a tarot card reader or astrologer to lend a touch of mystique to the occasion.

5. Masquerade Ball: A Masquerade Ball-themed gathering exudes elegance and mystery. Invite visitors to wear extravagant masks and fancy

clothing. As centerpieces, use luxurious textiles, candelabras, and masks to decorate the space. To create a classy and vibrant ambiance, use live music or a DJ. A red carpet entry and professional photographers may add glitz to the occasion.

6. Around the World: With an Around the World theme, you may take your visitors on a global trip. Decorate various portions of the venue to reflect other nations or cities, highlighting their distinct cultures and monuments. Provide a broad menu with foreign food and specialty drinks from various places. Cultural activities such as henna tattoos, Chinese calligraphy, and salsa dance instruction are available to guests, creating a festival that honors variety and discovery.

7. Hollywood Glam: Roll out the red carpet and celebrate Hollywood's glitz and glamour with a Hollywood Glam-themed party. Set the mood with a Hollywood sign, paparazzi-style photos, and movie-themed décor. Encourage attendees to dress up and provide a photo booth with props for entertaining photographs. Consider arranging an awards ceremony or a movie trivia game to engage attendees and generate excitement.

8. Tropical Paradise: A Tropical Paradise theme will provide your gathering with a flavor of the tropics. You can transform the location into a beachfront sanctuary with palm palms, tiki torches, and vivid flower arrangements. Serve fresh fruits, seafood, and excellent meals alongside tropical beverages. Guests are encouraged to wear Hawaiian shirts, sundresses, and flip-flops. To create a casual and joyous environment, including a live band playing reggae or steel drum music.

9. Fairy Tale Wonderland: Use a Fairy Tale Wonderland theme to create a fairy tale-inspired event. You can transform the venue into a beautiful realm with castle-like décor, shimmering fairy lights, and whimsical accessories. Invite visitors to dress up as their favorite fairy tale characters or in formal clothing appropriate for a royal ball. Provide engaging activities such as a princess makeover station, a treasure hunt, or a storytelling nook to immerse guests in a magical world.

10. Science-Fiction Extravaganza: With a Sci-Fi Extravaganza theme, you may immerse yourself in

science fiction. To decorate the venue, use futuristic features, neon lighting, and space-themed objects. Encourage guests to dress up like their favorite sci-fi or futuristic figures. Create interactive activities like virtual reality games, a laser tag arena, or a science fiction movie marathon.

These are just some of the ideas to get your mind and creativity going. The choices are limitless, and you can mix and match numerous themes to create a one-of-a-kind and fantastic party experience. The idea is to choose a piece appropriate for the event, reflect the host's personality or hobbies and provide visitors with an immersive and engaging experience. So, explore the world of themes, let your imagination run wild, and throw a party that will be remembered for years.

Considerations for Selecting A Theme

Choosing a suitable theme for your party is an extensive choice that may significantly impact the entire mood and visitor experience. While the possibilities may appear limitless, there are some elements to consider when choosing a theme to guarantee a successful and entertaining event. Consider some essential aspects while picking a theme for your next party.

1. Occasion and Goal: The first thing to consider is the party's occasion and purpose. Is it a birthday party, a graduation party, a work function, or a holiday get-together? The theme should be appropriate for the event's nature and purpose. A beach-themed party, for example, would be ideal for a summer birthday celebration, while a black-tie affair would be more appropriate for a formal business function. Consider the significance of the event and select a theme that complements it.

2. Preferences and Interests of Guests: Consider your visitors' likes and hobbies when choosing a theme. Consider your guests' demographics and what they might love. Do they have a favorite era, movie genre, or hobby? You may select a topic that connects with them and inspires excitement by studying their hobbies. This ensures that your attendees are involved and excited about the

celebration, making it a memorable experience for everybody.

3. Location and Setting: The location and setting of your party are essential factors in theme choosing. Consider the venue's location and physical characteristics. Is there anything special about it or architectural features that may be included in the theme? Consider the available area and how the theme will fit into it. An article that compliments the venue's mood will create a coherent and aesthetically appealing setting.

4. Season and time: The season and time of your party also impact the theme you choose. Consider the time of year and the weather conditions. A winter wonderland theme might be appropriate for a December holiday party, but a luau theme would be more suitable for a July event. Aligning the piece with the season gives a touch of relevancy and improves your guests' entire experience.

5. Budget and Resources: When selecting a subject, remember your budget and available resources. Some themes may have more extensive decorations, props, or specialist

services, which will influence your budget. Examine your available resources and decide what is achievable within your budget. Remember that a well-executed theme does not have to be costly. You can design a unique piece that meets your budget by being creative and resourceful.

6. Adaptability and Flexibility: Selecting a theme that provides flexibility and adaptability is critical. Consider whether the concept is easily adaptable to different age groups, tastes, or cultural backgrounds. This adaptability guarantees that all visitors may participate and enjoy the celebration regardless of their preferences. Furthermore, a theme for customization and modification allows you to incorporate one-of-a-kind elements that represent your style and ingenuity.

7. Accessibility and Inclusivity: It is critical to consider accessibility and inclusivity for all attendees when choosing a theme. Ensure the topic does not exclude or alienate people based on their talents, cultural origins, or religious views. Consider any sensitivities and select a piece that is inclusive and friendly to all attendees. This will promote a sound and inclusive environment,

encouraging a sense of belonging and ensuring everyone can enjoy the celebration fully.

8. implementation and Practicality: Finally, examine the practicality and simplicity of performance for your chosen subject. Check whether you have the appropriate resources, time, and help to bring the topic to life. If a theme necessitates complex props, complicated décor, or specialist services, be sure you can manage these components appropriately within your skills. It is critical to select a theme that you are confident in executing since this will add to the party's overall success.

By considering these elements when selecting a theme for your party, you can guarantee that you choose an appropriate option for the occasion, appeals to your attendees' interests, compliments the location, and works within your budget and available resources. A well-chosen theme sets the tone for a memorable and pleasurable event, resulting in an immersive and engaging experience for all attendees. So, investigate your alternatives, consider these aspects, and let your creativity shine as you design the perfect party with a theme that will leave a lasting impact on your visitors.

Examples of Inventive and Unusual Graduation Party Themes

Graduation is an important life event representing the culmination of years of hard work and devotion. Hosting a unique and imaginative graduation party may make this great moment even more memorable. Here are some examples of distinctive and innovative graduation party themes that will leave a lasting impact on your guests, from personalized pieces representing the graduate's hobbies to unique concepts that break away from established standards.

1. Travel the World: Create a Travel the World-themed party to take your guests on a globetrotting excursion. Decorate the venue with maps, bags, and other travel-related items. Set up stations depicting other nations, each with cuisine, music, and décor. Visitors may collect "passports" and obtain stamps as they visit each

station, offering an interactive and immersive experience.

2. Retro Arcade: A Retro Arcade-themed party will evoke memories and restore the allure of classic arcade games. Arrange for guests to enjoy old arcade machines, pinball tables, and foosball. Decorate with neon lights and vintage signs. Serve era-appropriate foods like popcorn, nachos, and soda floats. Guests can participate in high-score contests, which fosters a lively and competitive environment.

3. Outdoor Movie Night: With an Outdoor Movie Night-themed party, you can transform your backyard into a thrilling outdoor movie theater. Provide a giant projection screen, comfy seats with blankets and cushions, plus popcorn and drinks. String lights and lanterns may be used to create a comfortable environment. Choose a selection of the graduate's favorite movies or vintage films to screen, allowing visitors to enjoy a cinematic experience beneath the stars.

4. Game of Thrones: A Game of Thrones-themed party might be an incredible way to celebrate the graduation of fans of the famous series. To create

a medieval feel, use castle-inspired decorations, dragon props, and banners representing different households. Inviting visitors to dress up as their favorite characters and serving themed food and beverages are also encouraged. Organize activities based on the show's plot, such as quiz competitions or a scavenger hunt.

5. Time Capsule: Celebrate graduation with a Time Capsule-themed party. Please set up a special place for attendees to give objects that symbolize their shared memories and experiences. Set up stationery and prompts for visitors to write letters to themselves or the graduate in the future. Make a "capsule" to hold the gathered objects and seal them to be opened later, allowing everyone to reflect on their voyage.

6. Carnival Extravaganza: A Carnival Extravaganza theme will bring the vivid energy of a carnival to your graduation celebration. Set up game booths, a picture booth with props, and, if feasible, classic carnival attractions like a Ferris wheel or a carousel. Cotton candy, popcorn, and other carnival staples are available. Hire jugglers, acrobats, or stilt walkers to delight your visitors.

This motif ensures a cheerful and dynamic environment.

7. Homemade Crafts & Creations: Host a DIY Crafts and Creations-themed party for a more engaging and hands-on experience. Set up numerous creative stations so visitors can participate in activities like painting, ceramics, jewelry, and candle-making. For each station, provide materials, tools, and instructions. Guests may take their masterpieces home as one-of-a-kind party keepsakes.

8. Science Fiction: Take a trip into the future with a Science Fiction-themed graduation celebration. With metallic decorations, LED lights, and futuristic accessories, you may transform the venue into a space-age scene. Encourage guests to dress up like their favorite sci-fi or fantasy characters from movies or novels: present "galactic" cuisine and drinks uniquely. Incorporate sci-fi quiz games, virtual reality activities, or even a robot demonstration to enhance the theme.

9. Art Gallery Showcase: If the graduate is interested in art, throwing an Art Gallery Showcase-themed party might be a great way to

commemorate their accomplishments. They can display their artwork, pictures, or creative endeavors throughout the space. Set up several art stations so guests may paint, draw, or work on collaborative art projects. Make it feel like a gallery opening, with quiet music, hors d'oeuvres, and beverages.

10. Survivor Challenge: A Survivor Challenge-themed party will have you in the mood for adventure. Divide the visitors into teams and set up a series of tasks and obstacle courses for them to complete. Physical activities, cerebral challenges, and team-building exercises should all be included. To increase the sense of competitiveness, provide bandanas or team jerseys. Give incentives to the winning team and make memories of conquering obstacles together.

These unusual and innovative graduation party themes deviate from the norm and provide an opportunity to commemorate this occasion memorably and entertainingly. These themes allow the graduate and their guests to immerse themselves in a one-of-a-kind celebration that genuinely reflects their interests and hobbies, whether it's enjoying a favorite TV program, exploring new cultures, or promoting interactive interactions. So, let your imagination go wild, pick a theme that speaks to the graduate, and create a fantastic graduation party experience.

Chapter 4

Party Planning Requirements

Proper planning is critical when throwing a successful and memorable party. There are various crucial factors to consider, from planning the guest list to picking the appropriate theme and coordinating all the necessary details. Here are some essential recommendations and guidelines to assist you through the party planning process and guarantee that your event is a success.

1. Establish the Purpose and Theme: Begin by deciding on the aim of your celebration. Is it a birthday party, a graduation celebration, or a casual get-together? Choose a theme that matches the event after you have a precise aim in mind. A piece brings the event together and sets the setting for a memorable experience.

2. Guest List and Invitations: Make a guest list based on the nature of the event and the amount of space available. Consider the venue's size and the atmosphere you wish to create. Send out invites quickly through traditional mail, email, or online. Include any relevant information, such as the date, time, location, dress code (if applicable), and RSVP information.

3. Budgeting: Create a budget for your party and assign monies to components such as décor, food and beverages, entertainment, and any other services you may require. Maintaining a budget will assist you in prioritizing your costs and avoiding overpaying. Consider cost-cutting techniques like DIY décor, potluck-style food arrangements, or choosing less expensive entertainment.

4. place Selection: Select a place appropriate for the size and concept of your celebration. It might be your own house, a leased venue, a park, or even a beach. Consider accessibility, parking, and adequate amenities. Plan the layout, seating arrangements, and decorations by visiting the location beforehand.

5. Décor and Ambience: Select appropriate decorations that complement your concept to create the desired environment. Whether it's balloons, banners, table centerpieces, or lights, make sure your décor adds to the overall atmosphere. Pay attention to details such as table sets, floral arrangements, and signs to add a sense of elegance or excitement to the area.

6. Food and Drinks: Plan your food around the time of the party, your guests' tastes, and the theme. Determine if you will prepare the meal, hire a caterer, or host a potluck-style event. Consider dietary limitations and provide options to suit everyone's preferences. Don't forget to give a variety of beverages, both alcoholic and non-alcoholic, to accommodate varied tastes.

7. Entertainment and Activities: Provide a variety of activities and entertainment alternatives to keep your guests involved and amused. Depending on the nature of your party, consider hiring a live band or a DJ, organizing games or competitions, erecting a photo booth, or employing professional entertainment such as a magician or a caricature artist. Choose activities

that correspond to the subject and the tastes of your visitors.

8. Music and Sound System: Music sets the tone for any celebration. Make a playlist that fits the mood and tastes of your guests. Ensure you have a capable sound system or speakers to give clear and entertaining music during the event. If hiring a DJ or live band, communicate your preferences and offer them a list of must-play songs or genres.

9. Party timetable and Flow: Create a schedule for the party, including the arrival time, particular events or performances, meal or snack times, and any other highlights you wish to add. A well-organized timetable provides a seamless flow of activities and keeps guests interested. However, be prepared to be adaptable and flexible in the event of any unforeseen adjustments or delays.

10. Security and comfort: Put your guests' safety and comfort first. Make sure there is ample seating and facilities. Provide appropriate shade and weather protection if your function is held outside. Consider any unique requirements, such as accessibility for disabled guests. To guarantee the safety of all participants, if alcohol is offered,

arrange for designated drivers or other transportation choices.

11. Thank-You and Party gifts: Express gratitude to visitors by presenting thank-you cards or modest gifts. These small acts go a long way toward making a pleasant and long-lasting impression. Consider customized gifts that represent the event's theme or recollections.

You'll be well-prepared to throw a successful and memorable event if you keep these party planning fundamentals in mind. From the beginning phases of determining the goal and theme through the execution of the many aspects like invitations, décor, food, and entertainment, meticulous preparation and attention to detail will guarantee that your party surpasses expectations and leaves you and your guests with memorable memories.

Creating A Budget

Creating a budget is one of the most important aspects to consider while planning any event.

Whether you're arranging a small gathering or a large-scale event, a clear budget may help you stay organized, prioritize spending, and make the most of your resources. In this post, we'll look at the advantages of creating a budget for your event and offer some practical advice on designing and managing your budget efficiently.

1. Financial Management: Creating a budget allows you to get financial control over your event. It lets you decide how much money you're prepared to spend and distribute your resources accordingly. With a budget in place, you can prevent overpaying and ensure that you make sound financial decisions throughout the planning process.

2. Expense Prioritization: Making a budget allows you to prioritize your spending based on its value and relevance to your event. You may spend more on crucial components critical to your event's success, such as venue rental, food, or entertainment, while paying less attention to less urgent issues. This guarantees that you are maximizing your money and investing in the areas that will impact your event most.

3. Avoiding Debt and Financial Stress: Event planning may be expensive, and without a budget, it's easy to overspend and incur debt. By creating a budget, you may set spending limitations and avoid financial difficulties. This allows you to avoid unneeded stress and enjoy the occasion without worrying about the economic consequences.

4. Getting the Most Out of Your Money: A budget pushes you to be resourceful and get the most out of your money. You'll be driven to locate more cost-effective alternatives and better vendor arrangements. You may make more educated selections and get more bang by shopping around and comparing rates. This enables you to plan a memorable event without sacrificing quality.

5. Tracking costs: A budget may be used to manage your expenses throughout the planning phase. It helps you to monitor how much money you've spent, where your money has gone, and what costs are still due. This will allow you to make adequate changes, reallocate cash, and stay within your budgetary constraints.

Budgeting and Budget Management Tips:

1. Establish Your Total Budget: Establish how much money you will spend on your event. Consider your financial capability, the size and scope of the event, and your priorities. Set a budget appropriate for your financial circumstances, and be honest about what you can afford.

2. Determine Major Expenses: Determine the direct costs critical to your event's success. This might include venue rental, food, décor, entertainment, invites, and other significant expenses. Divide your budget into categories based on the relevance of each cost.

3. Research and Compare Prices: Research various suppliers and service providers to understand their prices. Compare prices, read reviews, and receive quotations to ensure you get the best deal. Feel free to bargain or ask for a discount. Being proactive in your search might result in significant savings.

4. Consider Hidden fees: Remember that your event may incur hidden fees. Examples are taxes, gratuities, shipping charges, and any additional

services you may desire. Include these in your budget to avoid surprises later.

5. Make a Spreadsheet or Use Budgeting Software: Summarize your spending using a spreadsheet or budgeting software. Include the expected cost of each item or service and the actual amount paid. This allows you to track your spending and compare it to your budget. It can also help you find spots where you might need to cut back or make changes.

6. Plan for Unexpected bills or Emergencies: It's always a good idea to set aside a percentage of your budget for unanticipated bills or emergencies. This safety net gives you peace of mind if unforeseen charges materialize.

7. return and Review Your Budget Frequency: As your event planning progresses, replace and review your budget frequently. It should be updated with any new charges or modifications you've made. This allows you to keep up with your money and make educated decisions based on available resources.

Remember that creating a budget means something other than limiting yourself or lowering the quality of your event. It is about being fiscally responsible and using your resources best. With careful planning, research, and monitoring, you can produce a memorable event that coincides with your vision while maintaining your cost constraints. So, take the time to create a budget for your event and get the benefits of financial management and a well-organized financial plan.

Putting Together A Guest List

Creating a guest list is essential to event planning since it sets the tone for the whole event. Whether you're arranging a small gathering or a massive celebration, the people you invite may have a big influence on the atmosphere and overall experience. In this post, we'll discuss the significance of generating a guest list and offer advice on creating an exciting and memorable one for your event.

1. Determine the Goal and Nature of Your Event: It is critical to understand the goal and type of your event before constructing your guest list. Are you throwing a formal dinner party, a casual get-together, or a special occasion? Understanding the goal can assist you in determining the correct number of visitors, the sort of environment you want to create, and the event's level of formality or informality.

2. Consider the location and Capacity: When constructing your guest list, consider the capacity of your chosen area. Ensure the room can comfortably accommodate the number of people you invite. Finding a balance between generating a lively environment and providing enough space for your guests to chat and walk around comfortably is critical.

3. Establish Your Budget: Your budget will significantly impact your guest list. The number of attendees you invite will directly influence many aspects of your event, including cuisine, seating, and even venue size. Determine a reasonable budget and distribute resources appropriately,

remembering that each extra visitor increases costs.

4. Prioritize Close Friends and Family: Prioritize close friends and family members on your guest list. These people have played an essential role in your life and deserve to be a part of your special day. Inviting loved ones gives a warm and intimate atmosphere and allows you to deepen the most important ties to you.

5. Consider ties and Connections: Consider your visitors' links and connections. Consider inviting people who have similar interests or are connected. This can encourage conversation, networking, and community among your visitors. Mixing diverse groups of individuals may result in enriching interactions and a vibrant and dynamic environment.

6. Consider Compatibility and Dynamics: While having a broad mix of visitors is crucial, consider their compatibility and dynamics. Ensure that your visitors' personalities and hobbies are aligned, which may lead to a more pleasant and pleasurable experience for everyone. Aim for a well-balanced guest list that reflects your ideals

and brings together people who will enjoy each other's company.

7. Consider the following practical factors: Consider the practical aspects when selecting your guest list. Take into account the age, mobility, and accessibility of all participants. If your event is intended for families, make sure there are activities and amenities for attendees of all ages. Consider any dietary restrictions or special adjustments that may be required.

8. Keep Your Vision in Mind: While there are many elements to consider when constructing your guest list, it should ultimately represent your vision for the event. Invite people who will appreciate and contribute to your vision if you have a specific theme or ambiance. Your guest list should align with your event's aim, resulting in an engaging and unified experience for everyone in attendance.

9. Send meaningful invites: Once your guest list is determined, take the time to send out significant invites. Make your invites unique by using conventional cards, digital invitations, or a combination of the two. Include any relevant

details, such as the date, time, and location, as well as any further information or requests. Making your visitors feel valued and appreciated immediately sets the occasion's tone.

10. Be Aware of RSVPs: As you receive RSVPs from your guests, keep track of them and update your guest list accordingly. This enables you to control the number of participants, make modifications as needed, and ensure an exact count for catering and seating arrangements.

Creating a guest list is an art that requires serious thinking, rigorous organization, and a clear vision for your event. You can create an atmosphere that encourages relationships, ignites conversations, and makes a lasting impact on your visitors by creating a broad and exciting guest list. So, take the time to build a guest list that fits the spirit of your event and invites people who will help to make the occasion memorable and pleasurable for everyone involved.

Selecting An Appropriate Location

When organizing any event, selecting an appropriate site is a crucial step. The location sets the tone for your event, generates the mood, and determines your attendees' entire experience. Whether you're arranging a small gathering or a large-scale event, the proper venue may make or break the event. In this post, we'll discuss the significance of selecting an appropriate site and offer some advice on choosing a place that will make a lasting impression.

1. Think About the Purpose and Character of Your Event: Consider your event's purpose and character. Are you throwing a formal gala, a casual birthday celebration, or a business meeting? The sort of event will determine the style and mood you want to create, and your location should reflect that vision. Consider if you require an indoor or outdoor area, the amount of formality, and any special requirements or constraints.

2. Establish the Capacity and Layout: Determine the number of people you anticipate attending and select a venue that can comfortably accommodate them. Consider the space's layout

and flow. Ensure enough seating, distinct sections for specific activities, and enough room for mingling and socializing. Your guests should be able to walk freely without feeling cramped or overloaded at the location.

3. Accessibility and Location: Consider the venue's location and accessibility for your visitors. Is it centrally positioned or conveniently accessible from different sections of town? Consider parking availability, public transit choices, and any special requirements or concerns for your guests. Choosing a venue in an accessible and convenient location will make it easier for people to get to your event.

4. Amenities and Facilities: Evaluate the venue's amenities and facilities. Is there enough restroom space, food choices, video equipment, or stage setups? Depending on the kind of your event, you may require exceptional amenities or technical assistance. Check that the venue can satisfy your needs and has the essential infrastructure to improve your visitors' overall experience.

5. Financial Considerations: Create a budget for your event and decide how much you'll spend on

the venue. Consider the rental cost, additional fees or services, and whether the venue fits your financial limits. It's critical to strike a balance between locating a location that fulfills your requirements and keeping within your budget.

6. Ambiance and Style: The venue's atmosphere and style are essential in generating the desired environment for your event. Consider the space's interior design, architecture, and general appeal. Is it consistent with the subject or emotion you wish to convey? Please choose a location that suits your vision, whether a modern and sleek vibe, a rustic and comfortable setting, or an elegant and sophisticated one.

7. Flexibility and Customization: Look for an adaptable and customizable facility. This allows you to customize the room and make it unique to your occasion. Some locations may have limits or limitations on décor, entertainment, or food options, so it's critical to confirm these specifics beforehand. Choose a site that will allow you to realize your artistic ideas.

8. Reputation and Feedback: Before making a final selection, look into the venue's reputation and

reviews. Look for testimonials to obtain a feel of prior clients' or attendees' experiences. Examine internet review sites and social media for comments and insights. A venue with a good reputation and many favorable reviews is more likely to provide a high-quality experience for your event.

9. Pay a Personal Visit to the Venue: Whenever feasible, pay a personal visit to the venue before making a final selection. This allows you to evaluate the actual area, see the layout, and understand the atmosphere. Take note of any potential obstacles or possibilities presented by the location. Meeting with the venue personnel in person allows you to ask questions, discuss your particular needs, and verify your solid connection and understanding.

10. Plan and Secure the Location: Popular locations are sometimes fully booked months in advance, so it's critical to begin your search and secure your favorite venue as soon as possible. This provides peace of mind that you have booked an appropriate venue for your event and can proceed with the remainder of your preparations.

Choosing an appropriate site is critical to making a memorable and successful event. You may pick a venue that corresponds with your vision and creates a fantastic experience for you and your guests by considering criteria such as purpose, capacity, location, facilities, ambiance, and price. So, spend the time researching, visiting, and carefully selecting a venue that will set the setting for a genuinely memorable occasion.

Distributing Invites

Sending out invites is a fun and necessary component of event preparation. It's the moment when you give a warm welcome and officially ask your guests to join you in celebrating your great event. The invitation establishes the tone, increases anticipation, and generates enthusiasm for the approaching event. In this post, we'll discuss the significance of sending invites and offer suggestions for making the process more exciting and memorable.

1. Customization is Essential: When it comes to invites, customization is essential. Please make a point of addressing each visitor by name, making them feel appreciated and noticed. Personalization entails more than simply adding a name to an invitation. Consider adding something unique, such as a handmade note or a small remark expressing your delight that they will be there. This modest gesture impacts and fosters a bond between you and your visitors.

2. Reflect on the event's topic or Style: The invitation is your visitors' initial introduction to the event's topic or style. Take advantage of this moment to establish the tone and develop anticipation. Create invites that match the overall ambiance or topic of your event. Whether it's a formal event, a casual gathering, or a themed party, the invitation should give your visitors a taste of what's to come and inspire enthusiasm.

3. Pay attention to facts: A well-designed and comprehensive invitation is crucial to express all the essential points to your visitors. Include critical details such as the date, time, place, and any particular instructions or requests. Check that

the typeface and layout are easy to read and that the colors and visuals complement the overall design. Attention to these aspects assures clarity and gives your invites a professional and polished appearance.

4. Select the Best Medium: Consider how you'll send out your invitations. Traditional paper invites exude elegance and formality, while digital invitations provide convenience and simplicity of dissemination. Depending on the event type and your attendees' tastes, you can choose either or both. Make sure the medium you choose complements the design of your event and makes it simple for your attendees to RSVP.

5. Create an Engaging opener: Your invitation's opener sets the tone and attracts your visitors' attention immediately. Use an intriguing and innovative beginning sentence to grab their interest and entice them to read on. Make sure it fits the essence of your event and creates a lasting impression, whether it's a humorous comment, a thought-provoking quotation, or a whimsical invitation.

6. Provide Specific RSVP Instructions: Encourage your guests to RSVP as soon as possible by offering clear directions on how to do so. Indicate the preferred means of RSVP, such as email, a dedicated website, or a phone call. Include a definite RSVP deadline to help you plan and make accommodations. Consider adding something unique, such as a meaningful remark or a prize for early RSVPs, to boost engagement and promote timely RSVPs.

7. Include Interactive Elements: Consider using interactive features in your invites to make them more attractive. This may contain a tear-off area for attendees to RSVP, a QR link leading to more event information, a video message, or even a tiny surprise within the envelope. These interactive components not only make your invitation more memorable, but they also provide a fun and exciting factor for your visitors.

8. Follow-Up and Reminders: After sending out the invites, follow up aggressively with your visitors and provide reminders. Send a polite reminder with a note expressing your eagerness to meet them at the event closer to the RSVP

deadline. This gentle reminder guarantees that your visitors remember to react and assists you in keeping track of the total number of guests.

9. Thank Your Guests: Thank your guests for considering attending your event. A simple thank-you note included in the invitation or a separate thank-you message indicates that you value their attendance and adds a personal touch to the invitation process.

Sending out invites allows you to make an excellent first impression, establish the tone for your event, and build excitement among your visitors. You can guarantee that your invites create a lasting impression and inspire enthusiasm for your forthcoming event by customizing them, reflecting the event's subject, paying attention to details, selecting the correct media, and integrating exciting components. So, let your imagination go wild as you create invites that genuinely reflect the essence and style of your event.

Choosing The Appropriate Date and Time

Choosing the proper day and time for your event is a critical choice that may significantly influence its success. It sets the tone for attendance, assures visitors' comfort, and enhances the whole experience. In this post, we'll discuss the significance of choosing the correct day and time and some suggestions for making this selection more exciting and memorable.

1. Think about the nature of your event: Begin by examining the type and goal of your event. Is it a formal event, a casual get-together, or a themed celebration? Understanding the core of your event can assist you in determining the best day and time. For example, if you're planning a business conference, weekdays may be preferred to accommodate professionals, while weekends may be preferable to accommodate social gatherings.

2. Investigate and Avoid Conflicts: Conduct a careful investigation to uncover potential conflicts or competing events before settling on a date and time. Examine municipal calendars, community schedules, and industry-related activities for

conflicts with your event. Avoid conflicts means that your event can avoid extra competition for guests and resources, increasing the likelihood of increased attendance.

3. Think about your target audience: The optimum date and time for your event are determined by your target audience. Please take into account their demographics, tastes, and availability. Evenings or weekends may be more convenient if your event is aimed at working professionals. Weekends or holidays may be preferable for a family-oriented event. Aligning the date and time with your target audience's schedule increases the likelihood of better participation and engagement.

4. Considerations for the Weather: Weather can affect attendance and overall event experience depending on location and time of year. When choosing a date, consider the climate and seasonal trends. If your event is held outside, decide when the weather is usually pleasant. If the event is indoors, be aware of extreme weather conditions that may influence travel or guest comfort.

5. Accessibility and Travel: It is critical to guarantee that your attendees can quickly attend your event. Consider your venue's location and the travel time necessary for your visitors. Choose a day and time that allows easy travel and minimizes conflicts with other obligations. Consider potential traffic or transportation issues if your event is scheduled during high travel seasons or holidays.

6. Cultural and Religious issues: Consider cultural and religious matters when choosing a date and time. Avoid arranging your event around significant holidays or religious observances since this may prohibit certain visitors from coming. Considering cultural diversity demonstrates respect and guarantees that your event is inclusive and friendly to all participants.

7. Consult with Key Stakeholders: Consider the availability of significant stakeholders or VIPs when selecting a date and time for your event. Contact them ahead of time to enquire about potential schedule conflicts. You exhibit respect for important persons' time and boost the

chances of their participation by incorporating them into the decision-making process.

8. Plan and Provide Notice: Once you've established the best day and time, give your guests plenty of notice. This enables individuals to manage their calendars better and enhances the chance of their attendance. Send out save-the-date reminders several weeks ahead, followed by formal invites or event announcements. Clear communication and advance notice assist your attendees in prioritizing your event and reducing disputes.

9. Flexibility and Alternatives: In certain circumstances, finding a date and time that works for everyone may be impossible. Consider providing alternatives or allowing for various possibilities. For example, if you're planning a multi-day conference, offer multiple registration options to let guests select the days that best suit their schedule. Flexibility displays your willingness to work with your visitors' schedules and increases their engagement likelihood.

Choosing the best day and time for your event takes careful thinking and intelligent preparation.

You can optimize attendance and create an engaging and memorable experience for your guests by considering the nature of your event, researching conflicts, understanding your target audience, factoring in weather and accessibility, being mindful of cultural considerations, consulting key stakeholders, planning, and offering flexibility. So, take the time to select the perfect day and time for your event carefully, and then watch as it unfolds effectively.

Chapter 5

Ideas for Graduation Parties That Will Leave You Speechless

Graduation is an important life event—a time of achievement, development, and new beginnings. It results from years of commitment, hard work, and many memories. What better way to commemorate this historic achievement than a stunned graduation party? In this post, we'll look at some unique graduation party ideas that will take your celebration to new heights and leave a lasting impression on the graduate and their guests.

1. Soirée Enchanted Garden: Turn your backyard into a creative and charming garden party. To create a beautiful environment, decorate the room with glittering lights, bright flowers, and lush vegetation. Set up comfortable seating spaces, attractive tables with floral displays, and a dance floor for guests to sway under the stars.

Ethereal decorations, such as hanging lanterns or fairy lights, add a sense of awe. Everyone will be transported into beauty and joy at this stunning garden soirée.

2. Retro flashback event: Host a retro flashback event that pays respect to the graduate's favorite era to take a sentimental trip down memory lane. Whether it's '70s disco mania, '80s neon extravaganza, or '90s grunge revolution, embrace the aesthetic and spirit of the decade. Decorate the venue with era-appropriate décor, play classical music from the era, and encourage attendees to wear retro garb. This throwback will create a dynamic and memorable party atmosphere.

3. Starry Night Gala: A starry night gala will transform your site into a heavenly fantasy. You may create a stunning ambiance using stellar backgrounds, glittering string lights, and celestial-themed decorations. Encourage visitors to dress up for the occasion and make a red-carpet arrival. Set up photo booths with heavenly accessories so that guests may snap breathtaking moments. Hire a stargazing specialist to provide an instructive

and awe-inspiring presentation on the night sky for an added touch of charm. Everyone will feel as if they are dancing amid the stars at this magnificent extravaganza.

4. Game Night Extravaganza: Bring out your competitive side and throw a fantastic extravaganza. Set up several gaming stations throughout the venue, with alternatives such as board games, arcade games, and even a mini-golf course. Create a dynamic and participatory atmosphere by awarding rewards to the winners. Consider including bespoke quiz games based on the graduate's accomplishments and memorable occasions. Everyone will be amused, laughing, and making new friends at this game night extravaganza.

5. Fiesta de la Cultural Fusion: Celebrate the graduate's multicultural roots with a cultural fusion feast with various customs and tastes. Create themed stations that reflect other cultures, with cuisine, music, and activities worldwide. Encourage people to dress traditionally and to enjoy the multicultural experience. Incorporate performances such as dances, music, or cultural

displays to immerse everyone in the celebration of variety fully. This bright and inclusive fiesta will foster community and admiration for all cultures.

6. Movie Marathon Marathon: You may transform your location into a comfortable and cinematic refuge with a movie marathon extravaganza. Create a relaxing lounge with luxurious cushions, bean bags, and blankets. You can create a nostalgic atmosphere with old movie posters and a concession stand selling popcorn, candy, and drink. Curate a list of the graduate's favorite films, or display a sequence that illustrates their path. Enhance the experience by inviting beloved figures to visit unexpectedly or hosting a themed costume contest. This movie marathon will create an intimate, engaging environment that honors the graduate's love of movies.

7. Adventure Quest: Embark on an exciting adventure quest that will take guests through difficulties, riddles, and surprises. Create a treasure hunt across the venue, with clues and puzzles bringing players to different spots. Include team-based activities and games that necessitate teamwork and problem-solving. You may create

an immersive setting using themed items, decorations, and hidden surprises along the route. Finish the journey with a big climax and congratulate the graduate on their achievement. After this daring celebration, Everyone will buzz with excitement and a sense of accomplishment.

8. Artistic display: If the graduate has a gift for the arts, why not hold an art collection that showcases their creative abilities? Create a gallery-style show of their artwork, photography, or performances. Make interactive art stations available so that people may make their creations. Incorporate live music or spoken word performances to provide another level of artistic expression. This creative presentation will honor the graduate's abilities while inspiring and encouraging innovation.

9. Beach Bonanza: A beach bonanza party will transport guests to a tropical paradise. Set up a beach-themed scene with sand, lounge chairs, and bright umbrellas. Provide cool drinks, tropical-inspired cuisine, and beach-themed activities such as beach volleyball or water games. Engage the services of a DJ to play cheerful music and create

a vibrant and dynamic mood. Remember to give your visitors sunscreen and beach-themed gifts to take home. This beach bonanza will bring the excitement and relaxation of a beach vacation to your graduation party.

10. Masquerade Ball: A masquerade ball will add mystery and elegance to your graduation party. Upon arrival, encourage visitors to dress up and gift them with wonderfully created masks. Decorate the location with luxurious textiles, lighted lighting, and lavish centerpieces. Set the tone with live music, a dance floor, and choreographed routines performed by professional dancers. This masquerade party will transport everyone to a world of elegance, intrigue, and beauty.

When throwing a fantastic graduation party, these ideas are only the tip of the iceberg. Allow your creativity to go wild, tailoring the concepts to the graduate's personality and hobbies and creating a one-of-a-kind and entertaining event that will leave everyone speechless. Celebrate this milestone with a celebration that respects the graduate's accomplishments and provides lifetime memories for those who attend.

Outside Extravaganza - Arrange an Outdoor Event.

There's nothing quite like embracing the splendor of the great outdoors to organize a graduation celebration that genuinely stands out. An outdoor spectacular provides a beautiful background for your festival and limitless opportunities for creativity and entertainment. In this section, we'll delve into the fascinating realm of throwing an outdoor graduation celebration, looking at ways to make your event a memorable spectacular.

1. Choosing the right site: Choosing the right spot is the first step in arranging your outdoor spectacular. Consider parks, gardens, roofs, or even large yards on private residences. Look for places with breathtaking vistas, plenty of areas for activities, and easy access for your guests. When conducting activities in public places, verify local legislation and secure the appropriate licenses.

2. Embracing Nature's Beauty: One of the primary benefits of an outdoor celebration is the opportunity to appreciate nature's beauty. Incorporate magnificent floral arrangements, vivid potted plants, and elegant decorations complimenting the outdoor ambiance to enhance the location's appeal. Use natural materials such as wood, stone, or straw to create a rustic and appealing environment that blends in with the surroundings.

3. Protecting Your Event from the Weather: While outdoor celebrations may be spectacular, it is critical to plan for inclement weather. Renting tents or canopies gives shade and protection from rain or direct sunlight. In case of poor weather, have a backup plan, such as leasing an indoor facility nearby or having a marquee ready. Depending on the season, consider hiring portable heaters or fans to ensure your visitors' comfort.

4. Captivating Entertainment: A spectacular outdoor needs enthralling entertainment selections. Set up engaging stations like picture booths with creative accessories, lawn games like gigantic Jenga or cornhole, or even a DIY cocktail

or mocktail bar. Engage the services of live musicians or a DJ to give a dynamic soundtrack that will keep the energy high throughout the event. Consider having outside events such as a dancing troupe, a live band, or a firework show to amaze your visitors.

5. Culinary Delights: The food and drinks you provide may enhance the outdoor experience. Set up a gourmet barbecue station with grilled favorites and delicious marinades. Set up food stations with various culinary alternatives, such as fresh salads, appetizers, and themed food bars, such as a taco or dessert bar. Consider working with local food trucks to provide a variety of cuisines and bring a personal touch to your event.

6. Lighting and Atmosphere: When the sun goes down, the correct lighting can turn your outdoor spectacular into a beautiful wonderland. Hide fairy lights, lanterns, or beautiful candles to create a charming ambiance. Colorful LED lights may be used to provide a lively and festive touch. Install spotlights to draw attention to certain places, such as the dance floor or entertainment stage.

The correct lighting creates an environment that will attract your guests.

7. comfy sitting: Provide plenty of cozy sitting alternatives for visitors to relax and enjoy the activities. Consider renting or arranging outside lounge chairs, picnic tables, blankets, and cushions for a calm and informal atmosphere. Incorporate pleasant lounging spaces with fire pits or outdoor heaters for chilly evenings. Remember to provide chairs for senior visitors or those wanting a break from standing and chatting.

8. Eco-friendly techniques: Demonstrate environmental stewardship by implementing eco-friendly strategies into your outdoor spectacular. Using biodegradable or reusable plates, cutlery, and drinkware decreases trash. Make recycling and composting stations available around the venue. Choose decorations and favors manufactured from environmentally friendly materials. By making eco-friendly decisions, you help the environment and set an excellent example for your guests.

9. Personalized Elements: Personalize your outdoor party to make it unique. Show a photo

collage or slideshow of notable moments from the graduate's life. Make personalized signs, banners, or flags with the graduate's name and accomplishments. Make customized party treats or mementos available for attendees to take home as a remembrance of the critical event. These unique touches will make your event seem more personal and meaningful.

10. Prioritize the safety of your visitors as you design your outdoor spectacular. To avoid accidents, ensure adequate illumination, clear routes, and signs. Make first-aid supplies readily available, and designate a specific space where visitors may get assistance if necessary. Communicate any safety instructions or regulations to your guests to guarantee a safe and enjoyable celebration.

You'll create a fantastic graduation party by embracing the outdoors and creating an outstanding outdoor spectacle. Every element adds to a stunning celebration of the graduate's achievements, from selecting the ideal venue to including compelling entertainment and personal touches. So, let your imagination go wild and embark on an outdoor adventure that will make this occasion memorable.

Glamorous Gala - Planning a Smart and Stylish Event

A magnificent gala is an ideal way to take your graduation celebration to new heights of elegance and refinement. A glamorous gala blends grandeur, sophistication, and a dash of excess to provide a memorable and polished event. In this part, we'll look at ideas and strategies for throwing a magnificent gala that will impress your guests.

1. Choosing a Location: Choose a setting that radiates refinement and charm to set the tone for a spectacular banquet. Consider magnificent ballrooms, luxury event facilities, or ornately designed historic sites. Look for locations with chandeliers, majestic staircases, or lovely outside gardens. The venue will be crucial in establishing the beautiful ambiance you seek.

2. Dress to Impress: Encourage your guests to dress to impress, whether it's a black-tie formal or a dress code that corresponds with the topic of your gala. Elegant dresses, smart tuxedos, and sophisticated formalwear are required for a magnificent gala. When visitors arrive and realize how much work has gone into their appearance, the tone is set for an excellent and classy evening.

3. Opulent decoration: With extravagant décor, you may transform your location into a setting fit for royalty. Table linens, chair coverings, and drapes should be made of luxurious fabrics such as velvet or silk. Incorporate metallic embellishments such as gold or silver for an elegant touch. Tables should be adorned with stunning centerpieces such as rich floral arrangements, crystal vases, or candelabras. You can use flickering candlelight to create a glamorous mood, and soft lighting, properly positioned spotlights. The décor should transport guests to a realm of refinement and elegance.

4. Extensive Dining Experience: A spectacular gala necessitates a palate-pleasing gourmet dining experience. Work with a professional caterer to

create a gourmet menu, including lavish meals that are tastefully presented. Choose a set dinner or a buffet with a variety of sumptuous selections. Ensure the cuisine complements the event's elegance, emphasizing quality ingredients and flawless presentation. Remember to provide a selection of beverages, such as creative cocktails, exquisite wines, and champagne, to honor the graduate's accomplishments.

5. Live Entertainment: Incorporate live entertainment that captivates your visitors to create an environment of refinement and enchantment. Consider hiring a live band or orchestra to deliver captivating melodies and enticing dance tracks. If you prefer a more modern mood, hire a competent DJ to create a mix of beautiful and lively music to keep the excitement high all night. You may even hire a renowned artist to give a live performance or a riveting stage show to wow your guests.

6. Red Carpet Arrival: Make your visitors feel like superstars by having them walk down a red carpet. Please set up a separate location for attendees to have their photographs taken as they

arrive, capturing the event's sparkle and splendor. To create lasting memories, consider hiring professional photographers or setting up a photo booth with fashionable decorations. This red-carpet experience will make your visitors feel like celebrities and add elegance to the event.

7. Glitzy Activities: Provide entertaining activities for your luxurious gala's subject. Consider holding a casino night with experienced dealers and gaming tables where visitors may try their luck at traditional casino games. To enhance the excitement, you may also incorporate a silent auction or a raffle with lavish prizes. Make a lounge space for guests to unwind and mingle in luxury, fostering private talks and friendships.

8. Pay attention to the minor things that contribute to the overall beauty of the occasion. Use personalized place cards, menu cards, or engraved party goodies to add a sense of refinement. Consider including a guestbook with a theme in which guests may leave emotional remarks for the graduate. Elegant signs, personalized napkins, and high-quality dinnerware will add to the glitzy atmosphere.

9. Memorable Exit: As the gala draws close, leave on a high note with a grand exit. To leave a lasting impression on your guests, consider a huge fireworks display, a dazzling light show, or a confetti-filled departure. Create a spectacular send-off that represents the grandeur of the event and keeps people talking about it long after the night is over.

10. Event Professionals: Enlist the assistance of skilled event workers to ensure the seamless implementation of your gorgeous gala. A committed team of specialists will ensure that every part of your event works well, from event planners to coordinators, caterers, and waitstaff. Their knowledge and experience with high-end events will help you to unwind and truly enjoy the beautiful gala.

A magnificent gala can create an environment of refinement and elegance that will impress your guests with careful preparation and attention to detail. From the location to the sumptuous design, superb meal, live entertainment, and spectacular departure, every detail contributes to an evening that honors the graduate's accomplishments. So, roll out the red carpet, prepare for an unforgettable evening, and let the glitz and glam begin at your graduation gala.

Retro Party - A Nostalgic Retro Party

If you want to take your guests on a journey through time for your graduation celebration, a Retro Blast from the Past theme is ideal. Take your visitors on a nostalgic journey through time, complete with prominent trends. In this section, we'll look at ideas and techniques for throwing a retro-themed party that will have everyone reminiscing and dancing the night away.

1. Select a Decade: The first step in organizing a Retro Blast from the Past party is to pick a decade as your inspiration. Each period has its style and trends, whether the swinging '60s, disco-filled '70s, neon '80s, or grunge-filled '90s. Choosing a decade can help you design your party and provide a unified and engaging experience.

2. Time Machine: Transform your party site into a machine that sends visitors back in time. Set the mood with era-appropriate décors such as antique posters, vinyl albums, cassette tapes, or movie memorabilia. Incorporate the decade's signature colors, patterns, and themes. Consider establishing themed lounges or places that depict various eras, such as a retro arcade or a psychedelic '70s den. The facility should invoke nostalgia and immerse visitors in a nostalgic environment.

3. Dress to Perfection: Encourage your visitors to dress retro and embrace the selected decade. Provide era-appropriate recommendations and inspiration to help people get into the spirit. Consider bell bottoms and tie-dye shirts for the '70s, leg warmers and neon for the '80s, and flapper gowns and fedora hats for the '20s. You could even have a costume contest and award prizes to the best-dressed attendees. The clothing selections will enhance the authenticity and pleasure of the throwback experience.

4. Iconic Music: Music is essential in establishing the scene and transporting guests back in time.

Create a playlist of chart-topping songs, one-hit wonders, and classic anthems from the chosen era. Consider hiring a live band specializing in throwback music or a DJ specializing in spinning retro records. Encourage visitors to dance and groove to the era's famous tunes.

5. vintage food and beverages: Incorporate era-specific food and drinks to provide a tasty touch to your vintage celebration. Investigate favorite meals and beverages from the chosen decade and modernize them. Serve traditional drinks such as martinis and margaritas and a retro punch bowl. Consider creating a themed food station with popular items from the time, such as sliders, tiny burgers, or finger appetizers. The gastronomic experience will complement the party's overall vintage mood.

6. Throwback Activities: Involve your visitors in throwback activities that capture the era's mood. Set up classic board games like Monopoly, Twister, or Trivial Pursuit for some friendly rivalry. Make a DIY photo booth with decade-appropriate decorations to allow guests to record memorable memories. You might even hold a dance-off using

famous dance routines from the time, such as the twist or the moonwalk. These activities will keep your visitors entertained and stimulate engagement while revisiting the past.

7. Retro Movie Marathon: Create a pleasant environment with vintage-inspired seats and organize a retro movie marathon, including films from the chosen decade. Choose cult masterpieces, beloved comedies, or landmark films from the era. Serve popcorn, snacks, and refreshments to visitors while they watch these movie gems. This movie marathon will immerse your visitors in nostalgia and create a comfortable and pleasant environment.

8. DIY Decorations: Use your imagination to create DIY decorations that match the chosen decade. Use vintage artifacts as centerpieces, such as old record players, vintage cameras, or retro toys. Display nostalgic words or quotations on retro-themed signs or light boxes. Hang string lights, disco balls, or neon signs to create a vintage atmosphere. Incorporate era-appropriate symbols or iconography, such as peace signs, lava lights, or

Rubik's Cubes. DIY decorations offer a personal touch and allow you to express your ideas.

9. Costume Photo Contest: Hold a costume photo contest to encourage attendees to show off their throwback attire. Please set up a photo booth with a classic backdrop and decorations where guests can strike their finest poses. Create a costume contest where attendees may submit photographs of their costumes and offer prizes for the most simple, imaginative, or amusing outfits. This contest will encourage your guests to dress up and provide a fun and exciting activity during the party.

10. Retro-themed Party treats and mementos: Send your guests home with retro-themed party treats and souvenirs to remember the great night. Consider small vinyl records, personalized keychains with the party's emblem, or retro-themed photo frames as party favors. These gifts of gratitude will remind them of the enjoyable throwback experience they had at your graduation celebration.

By embracing the nostalgia of a Retro Blast from the Past theme, you can design a graduation celebration that transports your guests across time. Every element will add to a memorable and immersive experience, from renovating the venue to wearing retro costumes, playing legendary music, offering retro-inspired food and beverages, and indulging in throwback activities. Prepare to dance, reminisce, and honor the graduate's accomplishments in a funky and vintage way.

Destination Graduation - Host a Graduation Celebration In an Intriguing location.

When celebrating your graduation in a genuinely remarkable way, why not arrange a Destination Grad event? This concept mixes the pleasure of traveling to an intriguing destination with the joy of graduating. Whether it's a tropical beach, a bustling metropolis, or a tranquil mountain hideaway, throwing your graduation celebration at a place adds adventure and produces lifetime memories. In this section, we'll look at ideas and strategies for throwing a Destination Grad party that will impress your guests and make your graduation party genuinely memorable.

1. Choosing a Destination: The first step in organizing a Destination Graduation celebration is selecting the ideal venue. When choosing a vacation, keep your interests, tastes, and budget in mind. Do you enjoy going to the beach? Choose a sunny coastal town with beautiful beaches. Are you a city lover? Choose a dynamic city with thriving nightlife and limitless entertainment alternatives. Are you looking for quiet? Seek out a picturesque mountain or lakeside getaway. The location should complement your party idea and provide unique experiences for you and your guests.

2. Make Accommodation reservations: Once you've decided on a place, make lodging reservations for your visitors. Depending on the size of your group, consider booking a block of hotel rooms or renting a vacation house that can comfortably accommodate everyone. Consider camping or glamping in gorgeous locales if you're feeling adventurous. Ensure that the lodgings are

easily placed near the party location and have facilities that meet the demands of your visitors.

3. Party Venue Selection: Select a party venue in the destination that reflects the location's character while providing a gorgeous background for your celebration. Consider a beachfront site with stunning ocean views for a beach resort. Choose a rooftop terrace or a fashionable event location with panoramic cityscape views in a metropolis. If you're in a gorgeous natural backdrop, look for a venue with picturesque scenery or tranquil gardens. Your graduation party venue should complement the destination and provide a memorable atmosphere.

4. Themed Decoration: To create a unified and immersive experience, incorporate the essence of the place into your party design. For a beach destination, use seashells, starfish, and tropical flowers. Use city skyline elements, neon lights, or prominent landmarks for a city party. Use natural materials such as wood, foliage, and flower arrangements for a mountain or nature-inspired celebration. The themed decor will transport your

visitors to the place while also improving the overall mood of the event.

5. Local Food and Drinks: Involving local cuisine and drinks is one of the delights of organizing a Destination Grad party. Investigate the destination's gastronomic treasures and incorporate them into your party menu. Let the tastes of the place show through, whether it's fresh seafood, regional delicacies, or street cuisine. To provide a whole sensory experience, pair the dish with local wines, specialty brews, or unique cocktails. This gastronomic adventure will bring authenticity and excitement to your event.

6. Cultural Experiences: Make the most of your trip by including cultural activities in your itinerary. Arrange for traditional music or dance performances by local musicians, dancers, or entertainers to delight your visitors. Cooking lessons, painting workshops, or conventional craft demonstrations are participatory seminars or activities highlighting the destination's cultural characteristics. These cultural encounters will captivate your visitors and leave them with tremendous respect for the location.

7. Exploration and Adventure: Organize adventurous activities and explore possibilities for your guests to take advantage of the destination's unique features. Plan a day of water activities, such as snorkeling, kayaking, or paddleboarding, if you visit a beach. Plan a guided tour of notable sights or a treasure hunt in a metropolis. Plan hiking expeditions, nature walks, or wildlife encounters if you're in a natural location. These activities will not only generate beautiful memories for your guests but will also help them to immerse themselves in the beauty of the region.

Personalized mementos:

1. Provide bespoke souvenirs representing the location and the occasion to memorialize your Destination Grad party.

2. Consider personalized souvenirs such as keychains, magnets, or photo frames that include the destination's name or landmark.

3. Make welcome packages filled with local treats or travel necessities for your guests to enjoy throughout their stay.

These unique keepsakes will serve as souvenirs of the event and remind your guests of the great vacation experience.

9. Transportation and Logistics: Plan and convey the travel and logistical elements to ensure your visitors have a pleasant trip. Give them specific information about transportation alternatives, such as flights, vehicle rentals, or local transportation services. Make a thorough agenda that includes the party schedule, extra activities, and recommended tourist spots. Provide advice or suggestions for local services such as restaurants, spas, or tourist destinations. By giving detailed information, you will assist your guests in navigating the place and making the most of their vacation.

10. Capture the Memories: Arrange for a professional photographer or a photo booth to capture the memorable moments of your Destination Grad celebration. These visual memories will be treasured for years, allowing you to relive the celebration's delight and excitement. Encourage your visitors to use a designated hashtag to post their images and experiences on

social media, creating a virtual scrapbook that captures the spirit of your celebration.

A Destination Grad party provides an excellent chance to celebrate your graduation. You'll create an unforgettable celebration that combines graduation joy with the thrill of travel by selecting the perfect destination, arranging accommodations, incorporating themed decor, indulging in local cuisine and drinks, providing cultural experiences, organizing adventurous activities, and capturing memories. So pack your bags, invite your friends and family, and prepare to go on an incredible trip of celebration and adventure at your Destination Grad party.

DIY Delight - Make Personalized Decorations and Party Goodies.

The DIY Delight theme is ideal if you're searching for a graduation party theme that allows you to express your creativity and personalize every piece. With this theme, you may create unique décor and party goodies to impact your visitors. In this section, we'll look at ideas and suggestions for throwing a DIY Delight party, where you can show off your artistic abilities and create a genuinely one-of-a-kind and unforgettable event.

1. Pick a Theme: Before embarking on DIY crafts, consider picking a theme that will connect your party's pieces. It might be inspired by your favorite colors, a particular pattern, or a meaningful symbol representing your trip. A theme will help guide your crafts and guarantee a consistent appearance and feel throughout the party.

2. Handmade invites: Begin your DIY journey straight away by making handmade invites. Allow your imagination to run wild as you create and customize each invitation. Consider utilizing decorative paper, stamps, ribbons, or even a handcrafted object representing your party's theme. Handmade invites signal your visitors that they are in for a unique event.

3. Create eye-catching banners and backgrounds as focus pieces for your celebration. Let your creativity go wild using fabric, cardboard, or paper as your canvas. To make it particularly unique,

paint or print personalized inscriptions, quotations, or the graduate's name. Hang these banners and backdrops in prominent spots to customize your party space.

4. Photo Booth Fun: Create a DIY photo booth area so visitors may take photos of themselves having fun throughout the celebration. Make a background out of streamers, balloons, or a picture collage. Include a table with props such as hats, glasses, placards, and other themed objects for visitors to utilize in their pictures to add individuality. Encourage your visitors to be imaginative and enjoy striking positions.

5. Handcrafted Centerpieces: Create one-of-a-kind centerpieces that complement your theme and personal taste. Use mason jars, flower vases, or recycled containers as a base. Fill them with fresh flowers, colorful stones, or little trinkets relevant to your theme. Incorporate images or meaningful quotes to add a personal touch. These handcrafted centerpieces will give your party tables a beautiful and personalized touch.

6. Make Your Party Favors: Make DIY party goodies for your guests to take home as

souvenirs. Make unique souvenirs that represent your theme or the graduate's accomplishments. Handcrafted keychains, personalized candles, or little jars packed with handmade snacks are all possibilities. Remember to put them in lovely packaging and include a genuine message of thanks.

7. distinctive beverages and snacks: Use your DIY abilities in the kitchen to create fabulous drinks and snacks for your guests. Experiment with new flavors, vibrant ingredients, and inventive presentation. Create personalized labels or tags to go with the beverages and goodies to add a personal touch. Your cooking abilities and the care that went into each item will wow your visitors.

8. DIY Table Settings: Create eye-catching table settings using DIY items. Personalize place cards, napkin rings, and tablecloth decorations by hand painting or drawing them. Use ribbons, twine, or natural materials such as leaves or flowers to add texture and appeal. Personalized table arrangements will make visitors feel unique while creating a welcoming and harmonious environment.

9. Interactive Craft Stations: Set up interactive craft booths where guests may let their imaginations run wild. Allow your guests to make souvenirs by providing art items such as paints, markers, or beads. These craft stations will keep your guests interested and offer them unique gifts to take home, whether painting canvases, creating personalized t-shirts, or making friendship bracelets.

10. Create a remembrance wall or guestbook where visitors may leave emotional remarks or recollections for the graduate. Set up a massive photo frame or a board where guests may write comments or stock images. This will be a lovely keepsake of the great moments shared throughout the celebration.

You can incorporate your particular flair and creativity into every area of your graduation celebration with the DIY Delight theme. From personalized décor, party gifts, and interactive craft stations to handcrafted invites, each aspect reflects your artistic abilities and adds a passionate touch to the event. So prepare to let your creativity go wild, collect your creative items, and start a DIY adventure that will make your graduation celebration unique.

Themed Food Fiesta - Delicious and Thematic Food Suggestions

Food is more than fuel; it can enhance every occasion. The Themed Food Fiesta concept is ideal if you want to inject some excitement and innovation into your graduation celebration. This notion relies upon creating a meal that not only delights the palate but also complements the theme of your celebration. In this section, we'll look at delectable and themed meal options to make your graduation celebration a gourmet feast to remember.

1. Choosing a Theme: Before planning meals, choose a theme that will drive your food choices. The theme will establish the tone for your food fiesta, whether it's a specific cuisine, a cultural festival, or a unique notion. When choosing a theme, consider your favorite cuisines, ancestry, or future goals.

2. distinctive drinks: Begin your food fiesta by serving various unique drinks corresponding to your theme. Experiment with colorful mixtures, garnishes, and one-of-a-kind glasses. These trademark cocktails will set the tone and start the celebration flowing, whether it's a tropical punch for a beach-themed party, a sparkling spritzer for an aristocratic occasion, or a mocktail bar for a family-friendly gathering.

3. Appetizer Extravaganza: Begin your meal celebration with tasty and bite-sized appetizers. Provide a variety of alternatives to accommodate varied tastes and dietary preferences. Serve small tacos inspired by Mexico, Asian-style dumplings, Mediterranean bruschetta, or a gourmet cheese and charcuterie board. These tantalizing nibbles will whet your guests' appetites and set the tone for the main dish.

4. Main Dishes Inspired by a Theme: Create a menu centered on major courses that emphasize the tastes and soul of your selected theme. Consider presenting a build-your-own taco or fajita station if you're planning a Mexican festival. Include a pasta station with a selection of sauces

and toppings for an Italian-themed party. A roasted pig or a range of tropical-inspired meals would be ideal for a Hawaiian luau. To amaze your visitors, think outside the box and get creative with the presentation and tastes.

5. Interactive Food Stations: Set up interactive food stations to provide a fun and engaging aspect to your celebration. Live culinary demos, DIY food bars, or hands-on activities can be featured at these stations. You may set up a sushi rolling station where guests can learn how to produce sushi rolls. A build-your-own pizza station or a DIY burger bar are other popular options. Interactive stations entertain your visitors and allow them to tailor their meals to their tastes.

6. Delectable Desserts: No fiesta is complete without a delectable selection of sweets. Use sweets that complement your theme, or get creative with dessert presentations. Serve cotton candy, popcorn, and colorful candy apples to a carnival-themed celebration. If you're throwing a Parisian-themed party, serve delicate pastries like macarons. Set up a DIY ice cream sundae station with various toppings for a fun and delicious treat.

Choose desserts that will provide your visitors with a pleasant and gratifying ending to the party.

7. Food Presentation: Besides the excellent flavors, consider how your food is presented. Make the dish aesthetically appealing using bold colors, garnishes, and creative plating techniques. Use thematic components in your presentation, such as seashells for a beach-themed celebration or arranging food in the style of graduation hats. Remember that appearance is essential in improving the entire eating experience.

8. Dietary Considerations: Consider any dietary limitations or preferences your visitors may have while organizing your cuisine. Provide vegetarian, vegan, and gluten-free alternatives so that everyone may enjoy the culinary delights. To assist customers in making educated selections and accommodating their dietary needs, correctly label the food.

9. Customized Menu Cards: Enhance the dining experience by giving customized menu cards highlighting your food fiesta's delectable selections. Include descriptions of each dish, emphasizing its distinct tastes and components.

Include fascinating facts, anecdotes, or tales about the meals to make it more personal. These menu cards will help your customers navigate the menu and give a sense of refinement to the dining experience.

10. Food Stations Décor: Make your fiesta more festive by putting thematic décor elements within the food stations. Use bright table linens, attractive decorations, or theme-related signage. For example, adorn the stations with tropical flowers, tiki torches, and bamboo accents if you're doing a Hawaiian luau. These aesthetically stunning settings will immerse your visitors in the gastronomic experience.

You can take your graduation celebration to a whole new level of culinary enjoyment with the Themed Food Fiesta concept. The cuisine will be the event's highlight, from creative drinks and delectable appetizers to theme-inspired main courses and interactive food stations. So put on your chef's hat, experiment with cuisines worldwide, and prepare to excite your visitors' taste buds with a fiesta of tasty and themed meals.

Extravaganza of Entertainment - Live Performances and Interactive Activities

A graduation party is a time to have fun, make memories, enjoy the company of loved ones, and celebrate academic achievements. The Entertainment Extravaganza theme is ideal for taking your party to the next level. This concept concerns presenting live performances and engaging activities to keep guests amused and involved throughout the event. In this section, we'll look at exciting entertainment alternatives that will turn your graduation celebration into a memorable spectacular.

1. Live Musical Performances: Include live musical performances to set the tone for an unforgettable celebration. Whether performed by a local band, a solo artist, or a DJ, live music provides an exciting and dynamic ambiance to your celebration. Choose artists who can appeal to various musical interests and genres to guarantee something for everyone. Live music will get your

guests on their feet and offer a memorable event, from exciting dance songs to deep tunes.

2. Delights on the Dance Floor: Make a separate dance floor for attendees to let free and show off their moves. Hire expert dancers or dance teachers to lead group dancing sessions or perform enthralling routines. Encourage your visitors to participate, learn new movements, and celebrate with you. The dance floor will be bustling with excitement and humor, whether salsa, hip-hop, or even line dance.

3. Interactive Photo Booth: Set up an interactive photo booth offering more than photographs. Provide attendees with props, costumes, and accessories that correspond to your theme, allowing them to turn into different characters or express their personalities. Consider using a green screen or digital effects to take visitors to other settings or imaginary realms. Your visitors will have unique souvenirs to enjoy long after the celebration, with immediate picture printing or digital sharing choices.

4. Magicians and Illusionists: Hire magicians or illusionists to give your graduation party a sense

of surprise and mystery. These expert performers will captivate your audience with mind-bending tricks, sleight of hand, and logic-defying illusions. A magician's presence will stun and engage your audience, from card tricks to notable stage performances.

5. Activity and game zones: Create engaging gaming zones and activities to keep visitors occupied during the event. Set up traditional carnival games like ring toss, bean bag throw, and balloon darts. Consider including life-sized board games like Jenga, Connect Four, or a personalized graduation-themed quiz game. These engaging games will foster friendly competition and give guests of all ages hours of amusement.

6. Comedy performances and Improv Shows: They say that laughter is the best medicine, and what better way to incorporate fun into your graduation celebration than with comedy performances or improv shows? Hire stand-up comedians or improv troupes that can offer hilarious quips and impromptu performances. Their wit and comic timing will create a vibrant

and enjoyable atmosphere that will have your guests laughing.

7. Art Interactive Stations: Set up interactive art stations to encourage your visitors' inventiveness. Canvases, paints, brushes, and other art tools should be provided so visitors can express themselves through painting or sketching. Hire a caricature artist to make bespoke caricatures of your guests on the spot. These artistic activities will entertain your visitors and give them one-of-a-kind gifts to take home with them.

8. Fireworks show: If your graduation celebration is hosted outside and under safety requirements, consider concluding the evening with a stunning fireworks show. Fireworks are a visual feast that will impress your guests and provide a spectacular grand finale to your celebration. Follow all required licenses and safety standards to produce a stunning performance that will leave everyone astonished.

9. Interactive Technology: Use technology to your advantage by introducing interactive components into your enjoyment. Consider virtual reality stations where visitors may explore immersive

worlds or participate in interactive activities. Install multiplayer games on gaming consoles to foster friendly competition. You may also integrate augmented reality experiences, which combine virtual and real-world situations to provide a new and futuristic type of entertainment.

10. Surprise Performances: Include surprise performances in your entertainment extravaganza to keep your visitors on their toes. This might involve flash mobs, surprise guest appearances, or even talent shows with your friends and family. Imagine everyone's joy as they observe surprising deeds happen in front of their eyes. These incredible performances add excitement and generate remarkable moments that will be remembered long after the celebration is finished.

11. Interactive Workshops: Provide interactive workshops where guests can acquire new skills or pursue hobbies. Workshops such as dancing lessons, food demos, painting workshops, or DIY crafts sessions can be organized depending on your topic. These hands-on activities delight your

guests and supply them with helpful information or a new passion to pursue.

12. Professional Performers: Consider employing professional performers such as acrobats, aerialists, or circus acts to take your entertainment spectacular to the next level. With their incredible exploits, delicate maneuvers, and jaw-dropping performances, these accomplished artists will leave your visitors speechless. Their talent and expertise will lend a sophisticated touch and wow to your graduation party.

13. engaging Roving Entertainment: Include roving entertainment to make your celebration more engaging. Stilt walkers, jugglers, or wandering magicians that mix with the guests and perform up-close magic tricks or hypnotic talents might be included. Roving entertainment adds a layer of surprise and engagement by allowing visitors to interact with the artists and become a part of the enchantment.

14. Live Art Performances: Include live art performances at your graduation celebration to provide an enthralling visual experience. Speed painters, who make magnificent artworks in a

matter of minutes; graffiti artists, who display their abilities on big canvases; and even sand artists, who create hypnotic narratives using sand animation, are examples of this. These live art performances delight and have a memorable effect on the audience.

15. Karaoke and Lip Sync fights: Use karaoke or lip sync fights to bring out your guests' inner superstars. Please set up a stage with microphones and a screen that displays words, and allow your guests to show off their singing or lip-syncing skills. Make a friendly competition out of it, and even offer rewards for the finest performances. The fun and delight you will experience while seeing your friends and family sing their favorite songs will leave you with lasting memories.

The options for the Entertainment Extravaganza theme are limitless. You will build a graduation celebration of laughter, awe, and entertainment by including live performances, interactive games, surprise acts, and fascinating seminars. Your guests will be enthralled from beginning to end, and the memories made during this event will be treasured for years to come. So, get ready to impress your guests and let the entertainment take center stage at your graduation party!

Tech-Savvy Soiree - Using Technology To Provide A Contemporary Spin.

Technology is an essential part of our lives in the digital era, and what better way to celebrate your graduation than with a Tech-Savvy Soiree? This theme embraces the most recent technology developments and incorporates them into every area of your party, providing your guests with a contemporary and cutting-edge experience. Let's look at how you may use technology to bring a futuristic edge to your graduation party, from interactive devices to virtual reality.

1. Digital invites: Send digital invites to kick off your Tech-Savvy Soiree. Instead of traditional paper invites, use attractive, interactive e-invitations that can be distributed via email or shared via social media platforms. To set the tone for your tech-infused event, you may modify

these invites with unique text, dynamic artwork, and linked videos.

2. Mapping of Projection: You can transform your party setting into a stunning visual experience with projection mapping. Using specialized projectors, you may imprint elaborate patterns, pictures, or films onto three-dimensional objects or surfaces. Project graduation-themed animations, personalized greetings, or even a slideshow of unforgettable memories from your educational path to create a magnificent visual display. Thanks to projection mapping, your guests will be immersed in an exciting and dynamic world.

Experiences using Augmented Reality (AR): Bring the wonder of augmented reality to your graduation celebration. Set up interactive AR stations where guests may uncover virtual components placed over real-world surroundings using their smartphones or tablets. You may, for example, put up AR photo booths where guests can pose with virtual props and characters or set up AR treasure hunts that bring visitors to secret surprises across the site. The options are unlimited, and AR will provide your visitors with a one-of-a-kind and unforgettable experience.

4. VR Lounge: Create a specialized VR lounge where guests may escape reality and immerse themselves in virtual worlds. Give guests VR headsets and games, activities, or simulations to try. VR will take your guests to other dimensions and give unique activities, whether soaring through space, swimming with dolphins, or riding a roller coaster.

5. Interactive Digital Displays: Design interactive digital displays that engage and delight your visitors. Allow visitors to interact with digital material such as photo galleries, interactive games, or even a virtual guestbook where they may leave comments and good wishes using touch screens or motion sensors. These interactive displays will give your party a futuristic feel while keeping your attendees captivated throughout the event.

6. LED Dance Floor: An LED dance floor may transform your dance floor into a captivating display. LED lights change colors and patterns in response to movement or music on these

interactive flooring. The pulsing lights will create a dynamic and exciting ambiance that will entice your visitors to hit the dance floor and groove to the music.

7. Tech-inspired décor: Incorporate aspects of tech-inspired décor around your party location. Add contemporary touches to tables, walls, or bar areas with LED strip lights. Consider adding digital gadgets, like small drones, robotic figures, or wireless speakers, into your centerpiece arrangements. These tech-infused décor elements will add to the overall mood while also serving as discussion starters for your guests.

8. Social Media Integration: Use social media to your advantage by incorporating it into your party experience. Make a unique hashtag for your graduation celebration and encourage attendees to post their most incredible memories on social media sites such as Instagram, Facebook, and TikTok. Create a social media wall or display where postings with the hashtag may be shown in real-time. This will not only increase visitor involvement but will also function as a digital

memory wall preserving the highlights of the event.

9. Tech-Inspired beverages and food: Extend your menu's tech theme by including tech-inspired beverages and food. Serve futuristic drinks with bright LED ice cubes or edible QR codes that, when scanned, reveal unique drink recipes. Offer molecular gastronomy dishes using revolutionary cooking techniques or 3D-printed sweets to surprise your visitors and give them a taste of the future.

10. Robot aides: Introduce robot aides to your graduation celebration to provide a touch of originality. These robotic companions will captivate your visitors and create a futuristic ambiance, whether a robot bartender dispensing drinks, a wandering robot photographer catching candid moments, or a voice-activated assistant answering guests' inquiries.

The Tech-Savvy Soiree concept combines technology, innovation, and entertainment. You may create a futuristic party experience by adding digital invites, projection mapping, augmented reality experiences, and interactive displays. The cutting-edge components and interactive technology will wow your guests, ensuring your graduation celebration is modern and unique. So, prepare to embrace technology and take your graduation celebration to the next level!

Community Giveback - Combining Celebration and A Charity Purpose

Graduation is a considerable achievement that culminates in years of hard work and devotion. Why not take this significant event further by giving back to your community? The Community Giveback theme allows you to blend the joy of celebration with the spirit of generosity, resulting if not only acknowledging your accomplishments but also helping those in need. Consider how you incorporate this profound topic into your graduation celebration.

1. Select a Charitable Cause: Choose a philanthropic cause that speaks to you and is consistent with your beliefs. It might be a local group promoting education, healthcare, the

environment, or any other significant cause. Investigate many organizations, learn about their aims and effect, then select one to help through your graduation celebration.

2. Fundraising events: Throughout the celebration, organize several fundraising events to generate donations for the chosen charity. Raffles, silent auctions, gift boxes, or even a specific space where attendees may make direct contributions might all be included. Make your fundraising efforts more innovative by offering appealing prizes or incentives to entice attendees to give generously. Making donating a part of your celebration encourages people to participate in the spirit of generosity.

3. Volunteer options: Besides fundraising, provide volunteer options for your guests to participate directly. Collaborate with the charity of choice to select particular volunteer initiatives corresponding to your celebration's subject. It may include arranging a book drive, putting together care packages, or staging a mini-service event during the festival so visitors can get their

hands dirty. This enables everyone to engage and work together to make a good change actively.

4. Invite a guest speaker from the chosen charity to share their ideas and experiences with your guests. This might be an organization spokesperson or someone directly benefiting from their work. Their presence and experiences will give your guests a better sense of the impact your party's contributions may have and will motivate them to participate beyond the event.

5. Silent dance: Make your celebration stand out by organizing a silent dance with a charity spin. Provide wireless headphones and various music channels instead of conventional speakers. Each channel can represent a distinct philanthropic cause, and guests can donate to the channel they want to listen to. Guests may enjoy music while actively helping for numerous reasons in this dynamic and enjoyable event.

6. Create a collaborative art project where guests may contribute their talents to a more significant collaborative creation. Allow guests to express themselves and leave their imprint by providing a large canvas, mural, and art equipment. This

group artwork, which serves as a sign of togetherness and teamwork, might be auctioned off or donated to a local community center or charitable organization.

7. Sustainable Party Practices: Incorporate sustainable party practices to demonstrate your dedication to the environment. Use environmentally friendly décor, biodegradable or reusable dinnerware, and place recycling bins throughout the site. During the party, you might even conduct a mini-workshop to teach visitors about sustainable behaviors they may incorporate into their everyday lives. By adding sustainability to your celebration, you are committed to positively impacting people and the environment.

8. Share the Impact: After the celebration, tell your guests about the impact of your community service activities. Send a follow-up letter or generate a post-event report outlining the total dollars earned, volunteer hours donated, and the specific activities sponsored. This expresses gratitude to your visitors for their contributions and reaffirms the good change made possible by their involvement.

The Community Giveback theme mixes celebration, appreciation, and social duty, transforming your graduation party into an occasion that transcends individual accomplishment. You may generate a feeling of purpose and have a lasting influence on your community by raising cash, volunteering, and raising awareness for a philanthropic cause. So, let us celebrate with compassion and charity and make your graduation celebration a force for good!

Graduation Sleepover - Planning An Unforgettable Overnight Party

Why not commemorate this milestone with a Graduation Sleepover as you say goodbye to your academic path and welcome the exciting new chapter ahead? This one-of-a-kind and unique concept takes the conventional sleepover concept to a whole new level, resulting in an unforgettable event for you and your closest friends. Prepare for a night of fun, camaraderie, and making lifetime memories. Let's look at how you plan a Graduation Sleepover that everyone will remember for years.

1. Select the Ideal Location: Choose a location that can handle your overnight party. It may be your house, a large backyard, a leased cottage, or even comfortable camping. When choosing a venue, keep the number of attendees and the activities in mind. Providing a warm and welcoming environment for an excellent overnight stay is critical.

2. Cozy Sleeping accommodations: Ensure your guests have comfy sleeping accommodations. Create comfortable sleeping places using air mattresses, sleeping bags, blankets, and pillows. String lights, fairy lights, and soft pillows may be used to create a warm and inviting ambiance. To ensure everyone has a pleasant night, consider offering individual overnight packages with eye masks, earplugs, and personal amenities.

3. Movie Marathon: Begin the evening with a movie marathon of your favorite flicks or a selection of famous graduation-themed films. Make a comfy movie room with bean bags,

cushions, and blankets. Pop popcorn, make movie snacks, and enjoy the beauty of movies while reminiscing about your high school days and looking forward to the exciting future ahead.

4. DIY Spa Experience: Give yourself a DIY spa experience. Create a spa station with face masks, nail polish, calming lotions, and essential oils. Allow your guests to unwind and pamper themselves by providing petite facials, manicures, and pedicures. This will not only refresh everyone but will also give an excellent time for bonding and female conversation.

5. Midnight Feast: A sleepover is only complete if there's a midnight feast! Prepare a delicious variety of finger appetizers, nibbles, and sweet treats for you and your guests to enjoy throughout the evening. Set up a snack section with various alternatives, including both delicious and healthful. Remember to add some childhood favorites that will bring back good memories.

6. Do-It-Yourself Projects: Make DIY activities to amuse everyone. Please set up a creative station where visitors may use fabric markers or iron-on graphics to customize their graduation hats or T-

shirts. You may also plan a memory jar activity where each visitor writes down a favorite memory or well-wish for the graduate and sets it in a lovely decorated jar. These hands-on activities will not only inspire creativity but will also be treasured souvenirs.

7. Scavenger Hunt: Create an intriguing scavenger hunt that takes your guests on a trek throughout the venue or nearby neighborhood. Make unique puzzles, riddles, and challenges based on your high school experiences and successes. The scavenger hunt will bring an aspect of adventure and friendly rivalry to the event, encouraging collaboration and generating memorable memories.

8. Karaoke and Dance Party: A karaoke and dance party allows you to channel your inner superstar. Install a karaoke machine or utilize a smartphone app with an extensive song library. Sing your favorite songs, dance like no one is looking, and celebrate your graduation enthusiastically and joyfully. You may even host a little talent show where each attendee exhibits their abilities and talents.

9. Storytelling and Reflection: During the overnight, take some time to reflect on your high school experience and share relevant experiences with your peers. Make a nice circle and light lights, and invite everyone to share their favorite memories, amusing tales, and future goals. This will strengthen your relationships and provide a sense of intimacy as you start on new adventures.

10. Breakfast Feast: As the sun rises and your overnight concludes, round up the festivities with a delectable breakfast feast. Prepare a range of breakfast items, such as pancakes, waffles, fresh fruits, and pastries. This final dinner together will serve as a symbolic start to the day and signal the conclusion of an outstanding graduation overnight.

A Graduation Sleepover is a one-of-a-kind opportunity to honor your accomplishments and improve your friendships. It allows you to spend quality time with your closest friends, reminisce about your high school days, and make new memories as you begin the next chapter of your life. So, prepare for a night of laughing, camaraderie, and unending fun at your Graduation Sleepover!

Ideas for Graduation Gifts

Finding the ideal graduation present may be both thrilling and challenging. It's a chance to congratulate the graduate on their accomplishments, recognize this momentous milestone, and offer them something to encourage and support them as they begin their next chapter. We offer graduation gift ideas guaranteed to wow, whether you're searching for a sentimental remembrance, a valuable tool for future pursuits, or a unique experience to commemorate your successes.

1. Personalized mementos: Make a unique souvenir to capture the essence of their graduation day. Engraved jewelry, bespoke photo frames, and monogrammed accessories are excellent ways to give a special touch. These meaningful presents will remind them of their

hard work and devotion, and they will cherish them for years to come.

2. Inspiring Books: Books can inspire, educate, and guide people. Consider giving a book corresponding to the graduate's interests, ambitions, or plans. A well-chosen book may be a source of inspiration and encouragement as they navigate their route ahead, whether it's a motivating self-help book, a career-focused handbook, or a compilation of inspirational anecdotes.

3. Technology Gadgets: Technology gadgets are usually valued in today's digital world. Consider giving the graduate a smartwatch, wireless headphones, or a tablet to help them with their education, career, or personal activities. These devices provide practical value and demonstrate your attention and awareness of their modern-day demands.

4. Tour Basics: Encourage the graduate to tour the world and try new things by giving them travel basics. A high-quality backpack, a rigid suitcase, or a multi-purpose travel organizer is beneficial as they begin their post-graduation adventures.

Combine it with a travel guidebook or a scratch-off map to arouse their wanderlust and spirit of experience.

5. Professional Extras: Gift graduates with beautiful and functional accessories to help them make a polished and professional impression as they join their careers. A high-quality leather briefcase, a stylish pen set, or a designer watch can improve their professional image and boost their confidence. These accessories not only serve a practical purpose, but they also represent their progression into the next stage of their profession.

6. Opportunities for Skill Development: Give the graduate a one-of-a-kind experience that allows them to learn new skills or pursue their interests. Consider a cooking lesson, a photography workshop, or a subscription to an online learning platform as a present. These experiences give opportunities for personal development and show your support for their ongoing learning and self-improvement.

7. Financial Assistance: Graduation is a momentous journey into adulthood, and financial

assistance is much welcomed. Contributing to their student loan payments, opening a savings account, or offering a gift card to a company or service that coincides with their future aspirations makes a significant difference as they negotiate the financial demands of post-graduation life.

8. Wellness and Self-Care: Gift the graduate things that encourage relaxation and self-care to help them prioritize their well-being and self-care. A deluxe spa set, a meditation app subscription, or a fitness tracker can help them feel better physically and mentally. Encouraging them to care for themselves at this transitional time is a thoughtful and meaningful present.

9. Personalized Stationery: In this day and age of digital communication, personalized stationery provides a sense of elegance and class. Consider customized stationery sets, embossed notepads, or monogrammed notebooks as a present. Handwritten letters, thank-you cards, and journaling allow the graduate to demonstrate originality and professionalism.

10. Gift Cards: If you need clarification on their distinct tastes or want to offer them the

opportunity to choose, gift cards are a safe bet. Choose adaptable gift cards for well-known businesses, restaurants, or online platforms that appeal to various interests. This enables the graduate to choose what they desire or to partake in an experience of their own.

Remember that the intention and heart behind a graduation present is the most significant component. Consider the graduate's personality, objectives, and future plans when choosing a present. Whether you select an emotional souvenir, a helpful tool, or a memorable experience, your thoughtful gift will serve as a lasting reminder of their accomplishments and the support they have received.

Celebrate the graduate's achievements with a gift that symbolizes their unique talents, motivates their future pursuits, and demonstrates your appreciation for their hard work. Whatever you decide, your thoughtful gift will impact and contribute to their continuing success.

Congratulations, and may your present symbolize their tremendous and exciting future!

Chapter 6

Success Planning

Your graduation party is more than simply a party; it reflects your journey, accomplishments, and the exciting future that awaits you. Careful planning is required to guarantee that your party is a spectacular success. You can create a fantastic experience for yourself and your guests by planning and organizing every part of your event. Let's get into the essentials of arranging a successful graduation celebration and making it an occasion to remember.

Define Your Vision: Begin by defining your party's vision. What kind of environment do you want to create? What feelings do you want your visitors to feel? Consider the general theme, mood, and tone you wish to establish. Create a mental image of your perfect party and use it as a guide throughout the planning process. This clarity will assist you in making decisions and realizing your vision.

Making a Thorough Party Schedule

To create a perfect and memorable celebration, planning a graduation party entails juggling several chores, arranging suppliers, and managing diverse parts. A thorough party timeline is one of the most powerful tools. This timeline will act as your road map, leading you through each phase of the planning process and assisting you in remaining organized and focused. Let's look at the significance of a precise party timetable and how you may make one to ensure an extraordinary celebration from beginning to end.

1. Setting Priorities: Determine your top priorities and primary responsibilities. Determine the essential parts of your graduation celebration, such as venue selection, invitation distribution, cuisine preparation, décor setup, entertainment booking, etc. Prioritize these chores according to

their relevance and timeframes, first addressing the most critical areas.

2. Establishing Milestones: Divide your party planning process into defined milestones. These milestones indicate essential steps in your planning process and act as anchor points for your timeline. Booking the venue, completing the guest list, buying decorations, verifying the cuisine, and sending out invites are all examples of milestones. Set realistic deadlines for each milestone, allowing enough time to fulfill the related activities.

3. Going Backwards: Work backward from your graduation party date to build an efficient timeline. Consider the time necessary to accomplish each work and allow for eventualities. Begin by determining when the last chores must be done, such as décor setup, meal preparation, and guest arrival. Then, work your way backward, considering the time required for each previous step, such as meal planning, vendor coordination, and invitation mailing.

4. Task Breakdown: Once you've defined your milestones and the order of activities, break each task down into smaller, achievable chunks. For

example, under the milestone "Menu Planning," you may add actions such as investigating catering possibilities, deciding on a menu, receiving quotations, and finalizing the menu. Breaking projects into smaller sections makes them easier to handle and allows for more accurate time prediction.

5. Assigning Timeframes: On your timeline, assign exact timeframes to each job and subtask. Be realistic about the difficulty and length of each activity. Consider any dependencies or requirements that may affect the time of specific actions. You can observe the evolution of your planning journey and identify possible bottlenecks or locations where designated deadlines may require further help.

6. Allowing for unforeseen Delays or obstacles: Allowing for unexpected delays or blocks throughout the planning phase is critical. Allow some wiggle room in your schedule by including buffer times between tasks or milestones. This extra time can be used to deal with unexpected events, make revisions, or address last-minute alterations.

7. Using Technology and Tools: Use technology and planning tools to build and manage your party timetable properly. Online calendars, project management tools, and even basic spreadsheet programs may assist you in staying organized, setting reminders, and tracking progress. Consider adding visual tools such as color-coded timelines or Gantt charts to make your planning process more exciting and aesthetically attractive.

8. Reviewing and Updating regularly: A party timeline is not set. As your planning continues, evaluating and adjusting your timetable is critical. Check off completed tasks, make any necessary adjustments to deadlines, and account for any changes in conditions. You can stay on track and respond to unexpected changes by regularly evaluating and revising your timetable.

Your secret weapon for effective graduation party planning is a comprehensive party timetable. It gives you structure, clarity, and organization, helping you to handle many activities and deadlines easily. You can easily traverse the planning process and ensure a flawless celebration from start to end by creating priorities, assigning milestones, and allocating timeframes. So, take a pen, make a timeline, and start counting down to a memorable graduation celebration!

Making Preparations for Décor, Catering, and Entertainment

A good graduation celebration entails more than simply the location and guest list. The attention to detail, the ambiance, the enticing cuisines, and the enthralling entertainment elevate an ordinary gathering to a fantastic occasion. Making the arrangements for décor, cooking, and joy is critical to creating a memorable celebration. Let's delve into event planning and see how you can take your graduation celebration to the next level.

1. Enchanting Decorations: Decorations set the tone for your party, creating an ambiance that represents your individuality and adds a magical touch to the occasion. Consider your theme or color palette and choose decorations that complement it. Allow your creativity to run wild

with vivid balloons, exquisite centerpieces, sophisticated table linens, bespoke banners, picture backgrounds, and innovative lighting. Be aware of the minor elements, such as signs, flower arrangements, and creative table sets, which will impact your visitors.

2. Delectable Catering: Food is an essential aspect of every celebration, and catering may help you please your visitors' taste buds. Investigate several catering choices that fit your budget and tastes. Choose a menu that offers a range of flavors and satisfies diverse dietary demands, such as buffet-style spreads, sit-down dinners, or food stations with varied cuisines. To enhance the culinary experience, consider adding interactive components such as live cooking stations, build-your-own stations, or food trucks. Don't forget to add a range of alcoholic and non-alcoholic beverages to match the food.

3. Entertainment Extravaganza: The lifeblood of a memorable party is entertainment. Consider your guests' hobbies and preferences while selecting entertainment to keep them involved and amused throughout the event. Whether performed by a

band or a single performer, live music can create a lively and exciting atmosphere. Hiring a DJ guarantees a mix suited to your preferences and keeps the dance floor hopping. Consider employing professional dancers or entertainers who may captivate your visitors with their talent for a touch of class. If you want to add a one-of-a-kind touch, consider a photo booth, interactive activities, or a surprise performance or special guest appearance.

4. Audiovisual Improvements: Use audiovisual components to enhance the visual experience of your graduation party. Consider employing a lighting designer to create fantastic lighting effects that complement the atmosphere and concept of your event. Personalized slideshows or films highlighting your journey and successes may be displayed on projectors and displays. Use sound equipment to provide clear audio during speeches, concerts, and announcements. These audiovisual additions offer a professional touch and improve customers' overall experience.

5. Professional Services: Depending on the size of your graduation celebration, you may need to hire

specialists to help with various parts. Event planners may help with overall coordination by ensuring that every element is thoroughly planned and performed. Professional decorators can make your concept a reality and convert your venue into a stunning place. Catering services may manage all aspects of meal preparation, serving, and cleanup, enabling you to focus on having fun during the party. You may relax and confidently commit the crucial parts of your celebration to experienced hands by engaging the skills of specialists.

6. Personal Touches: While the significant picture components like décor, cuisine, and entertainment are vital, don't forget to include personal touches representing your style and personality. Include pieces highlighting your accomplishments, such as a display of certificates and honors or a memory wall with images and significant experiences from your educational path. Include personalized souvenirs or mementos for your guests to take home as a thank-you. These personal touches distinguish your graduation celebration and foster a stronger bond with your guests.

Remember to balance originality, functionality, and customization while planning décor, cuisine, and entertainment preparations. Allow your imagination to run wild, but keep reality and financial limits in mind. Finally, it's about providing an outstanding experience for you and your guests, with every detail meticulously planned and performed. So, prepare to awe your visitors with stunning decorations, tantalize their taste buds with delicious cuisine, and captivate them with fantastic entertainment. Your graduation celebration will be remembered for many years to come.

Managing Logistics and Coordination On The Event Day

The big day has finally arrived for your graduation celebration. As you prepare to celebrate this momentous milestone with your loved ones, excitement fills the air. However, in the middle of the excitement and expectation, it's critical to maintain a close watch on logistics and coordination to ensure that everything goes as planned. Managing these areas will help you and your visitors have a flawless and enjoyable experience. Let's look at some crucial strategies for handling logistics and coordination on the event day.

1. Making a Checklist: A thorough checklist will guide you on the event day. Make a complete list that includes chores like decorating, working with vendors, finishing last-minute details, and ensuring all required supplies are available. Prioritize projects based on their importance and delegate duties to trustworthy personnel who can assist you in carrying them out. Following a checklist will provide a clear roadmap of what must be done, limiting the possibility of neglecting crucial components.

2. Appointing a Point of Contact: Designate a point of contact for the event day, someone who will handle logistics, resolve difficulties, and, if required, work with suppliers. This individual should be thoroughly aware of the event's specifics, such as the timetable, layout, and special requirements. A dedicated point of contact

helps you enjoy the festivities while ensuring that any unanticipated issues are quickly addressed.

3. Venue Setup and Décor: Arrive early at the venue to supervise the setup and verify that the decorations are properly positioned. Coordination with venue personnel or decorators is required to ensure everything, from table arrangements and signs to lighting and video equipment, is in place. Check that the seating arrangement can handle the number of people planned. The detail-oriented setting will create an inviting and visually appealing environment for your guests.

4. Vendor Coordination: Keep open lines of contact with suppliers you've contracted for food, entertainment, or other services throughout the day. Ensure they are informed of the event's timeframe and any adjustments or specific requirements.

Confirm arrival times and setup instructions with entertainers or performers, and ensure they have everything they need for their performances. Effective vendor coordination ensures that all participants have a consistent and synchronized experience.

5. Guest Registration and Arrival: As visitors begin to arrive, make their arrival as easy and friendly as possible. Set up a registration area so visitors may check in, obtain name tags, and collect any required supplies or favors. Allow a team member or volunteer to meet attendees and advise them about the event layout, activities, and special announcements. Creating a welcoming and well-organized registration procedure sets the tone for the remainder of the event.

6. Transitions and Event Timeline: Monitor the event timetable to verify that each action and transition occurs as planned. Maintain flexibility, but stick to the timeline to minimize delays or confusion. Use visual cues, such as signage or announcements, to direct people through the event. Ensure transitions between speeches, performances, or other crucial moments are seamless, allowing for an efficient flow and keeping attendees interested.

7. Problem-Solving and Adaptability: Unexpected obstacles may develop during the event, despite thorough planning. It is critical to remain calm, think quickly on your feet, and overcome any

complications that may arise. Prepare for anticipated disruptions like technological issues or changes in weather conditions for outdoor activities. Contact your point of contact, vendors, and important team members to handle any concerns immediately. Your capacity to problem-solve and adjust in real-time will ensure that everyone engaged has a positive experience.

8. Interacting with visitors: While managing logistics and coordination, remember to interact with your visitors and enjoy the festivities. Take the time to meet and communicate with each attendee, and convey your appreciation for their attendance. Reconnect with friends, family, and mentors who have helped you. You will contribute to an environment of pleasure and celebration by making significant relationships and moments of gratitude.

Remember that handling logistics and organization is critical for a successful graduation celebration on the day of the event. You'll create a smooth and faultless experience for yourself and your visitors by remaining organized, communicating efficiently, and resolving any emerging difficulties. Accept the celebration, savor the moments, and rejoice in attaining this key life milestone.

Chapter 7

Graduation Party Planning Tips

The effort of planning a graduation celebration may be both exhilarating and intimidating. It's critical to make the celebration seamless and stress-free for you and your guests as you seek to create a memorable event that honors your accomplishments. You can arrange a graduation celebration that goes smoothly and makes a lasting impression with careful planning and attention to detail. Here are some helpful hints to get you started:

1. Begin Early: When preparing for a successful graduation celebration, time is your biggest ally. Begin your planning early, leaving plenty of time for organizing, making bookings, and sending out invites. If you start early, you'll have more flexibility in obtaining your desired location and

vendors and ensuring all required arrangements are in place.

2. Create a Realistic Budget: A budget is an essential stage in event preparation. Determine your budget and distribute it judiciously to various components like venue rental, décor, food, and entertainment. Remember to include any unexpected or hidden charges. Setting a realistic budget allows you to make educated decisions while avoiding overpaying.

3. Simplify the Menu: Regarding catering, simplicity is often the key to a successful event. Consider a buffet-style or family-style lunch that includes a range of foods and caters to several dietary requirements. Choose finger foods, appetizers, and self-serve stations that allow visitors to socialize and eat at their speed. Maintain a limited menu and prioritize quality over quantity.

4. Assign Responsibilities: You don't have to do everything yourself. Delegate responsibilities to trustworthy friends, family members, or paid specialists who can help with various facets of the celebration. Assign someone to be in charge of

the decorations, the music playlist, or the registration table. You may reduce stress and guarantee that each section of the party receives the attention it deserves by sharing tasks.

5. Prepare for Bad Weather: If you're planning an outdoor graduation celebration, prepare a backup plan in case of inclement weather. Renting a tent or renting an inside location as a backup plan may bring peace of mind and guarantee that the celebration goes off without a hitch, rain, or shine. Inform your guests of the backup plan beforehand so they know of any adjustments or venue shifts.

6. Consider the structure and Flow of the Party: To create a smooth experience for your visitors, consider the structure and flow of your party. Arrange sitting sections, food kiosks, and entertainment zones logically to provide seamless transitions and simple navigation. Avoid active regions and bottlenecks that might slow you down. Strategically placed signs or signage can also assist attendees in locating crucial parts of the celebration.

7. Create a timetable: Create a detailed schedule detailing the order of events and activities that

will occur throughout the party. Include actual events like speeches, performances, and any unusual surprises. Inform your vendors, volunteers, and critical personnel to organize the timetable. A well-organized agenda keeps everyone informed and ensures that every aspect of the celebration runs well.

8. Include Interactive Elements: Engage your guests by integrating interactive components that make the gathering more enjoyable and memorable. Consider a picture booth with props, a memory wall for attendees to leave comments or well wishes, or a unique guestbook for them to share their memories. These interactive features delight your visitors and serve as keepsakes of the event.

9. Provide Plenty of Parking and Transportation Options: If your graduation celebration includes parking, reserve enough space for your guests automobiles. Consider having information on neighboring parking lots or alternate transportation choices, such as shuttle services or ride-sharing programs. By planning ahead of time

for parking and transportation, you may eliminate potential logistical issues on the day of the event.

10. Relax and Enjoy: With all the preparation and coordination, standing back and enjoying the moment is essential. Remember that the purpose of this celebration is to acknowledge your accomplishments while also enjoying the company of your loved ones. Please take the opportunity to chat with visitors, exchange tales, and express your thanks for their assistance. Relax, take in the scenery, and commemorate this momentous day in your life.

Following these guidelines, you can arrange a flawless graduation celebration that makes a lasting impression on your guests. Remember that the keys to success are rigorous planning, good communication, and attention to detail. Enjoy the festivities, make lovely memories, and bask in the glory of your accomplishments.

Maintaining A Dynamic and Exciting Atmosphere

Graduation parties are occasions for celebration, fun, and the creation of lifetime memories. To ensure that your event is a rousing success, keep the environment alive and engaging throughout the festival. You may improve the experience for both you and your guests by including energy, excitement, and interactive components in your party. Let's look at some enticing ideas for keeping the environment lively and ensuring an outstanding party.

1. Make a Dynamic Playlist: Music is a vital instrument for setting the mood and energizing the audience. Make a playlist of your favorite music, big hits, and cheerful tracks to get everyone moving. Consider including various genres to appeal to different preferences and generations. If feasible, hire a DJ or live band to improve the mood and keep the celebration going.

2. Interactive Games and Activities: Incorporate interactive games and activities into your graduation celebration to add fun and friendly rivalry. Create a gaming zone with traditional games like cornhole, gigantic Jenga, or a picture

treasure hunt. You may also have friendly competitions such as karaoke, trivia, or a dance-off. These activities entertain your visitors and promote interaction and a dynamic atmosphere.

3. Use Social Media: Use social media to engage your visitors and extend the celebration beyond the event. Create a unique hashtag for your graduation celebration and encourage guests to post their images and experiences on social media channels like Instagram, Facebook, and Twitter. Consider setting up a social media photo booth section where visitors can shoot selfies and upload them directly online. This keeps the party going and generates a digital memory album for everyone to enjoy.

4. Surprising amusement: Surprise your guests with unexpected moments of entertainment throughout the celebration. Consider employing magicians, acrobats, or dancers to dazzle the audience with their abilities and charm. Surprise musical performances, flash mobs, or special guest appearances may add excitement and keep the environment charged.

5. Engaging Food and Drink Stations: Food and drink stations may function as participatory experiences in addition to satisfying hunger and thirst. Set up stations where visitors can create cuisines, such as build-your-own taco stations, DIY dessert stations, or interactive cocktail bars. As people congregate around these interactive stations, it allows customers to connect with the food and drink options, adds a personal touch, and creates a dynamic atmosphere.

6. engaging Photo Opps: Capture the atmosphere of your graduation party by hiring photo ops. Create personalized photo booths with accessories and backdrops that represent your personality or your celebration's topic. Encourage visitors to snap memorable images and give souvenirs such as quick prints or digital copies. These picture ops generate laughter and conversation and give physical mementos of the celebration.

7. Incorporate Personal Touches: Incorporate personal touches into your graduation celebration to make it genuinely memorable. Show a slideshow or video montage of noteworthy events

from your educational experience. Include moving speeches or tributes from friends, relatives, and mentors. These personal touches engage the participants' emotions, establish a sense of connection, and give dimension to the ambiance.

8. Surprise Giveaways and Prizes: Incorporate surprise giveaways and prizes throughout the celebration to keep the excitement levels high. Organize raffles, quiz competitions, or random draws where attendees can win fantastic gifts. These shocks add to the suspense and inspire active involvement and engagement.

9. theme Décor and Lighting: Use innovative and theme decorations and lighting to create a dynamic ambiance. To change the area and create an immersive experience, use bold colors, eye-catching centerpieces, and innovative lighting setups. To make the décor genuinely indicative of your journey, use things linked to your graduation theme or personal hobbies.

Finally, don't be hesitant to embrace spontaneity at your graduation celebration. Allow for unexpected remarks, surprise performances, or spontaneous dancing. Allow your visitors to have fun, exchange tales, and enjoy the freedom of the celebration. These unexpected moments frequently become the event's highlights, adding excitement and ensuring that the environment remains alive and engaging.

Combining these ideas into your graduation celebration creates a dynamic, engaging, and joyous atmosphere. Remember that the idea is to incorporate energy, engagement, and surprises into all aspects of the event. Allow the environment to reflect the great success and thrill of the voyage as you commemorate this momentous milestone.

Ensuring guests' Comfort and Delight

One of the most crucial aspects to consider when throwing a graduation celebration is the comfort and satisfaction of your guests. Your loved ones, friends, and mentors have gathered to celebrate your accomplishments, and it's critical that you create an atmosphere that makes them feel welcomed, appreciated, and at ease. You may improve the whole experience and leave a lasting impression by concentrating on their comfort and satisfaction. Here are some helpful hints for ensuring your guests' comfort and enjoyment:

1. Plenty of seating and lounging areas: Provide adequate seating and lounge places to accommodate your guests. Arrange chairs, sofas, and outdoor seats in distinct locations to promote relaxation and socialization. Make comfy nooks or discussion areas for people to congregate and have great talks. Comfortable seating arrangements demonstrate that you have considered your visitors' requirements and guarantee they can enjoy the party without feeling overwhelmed.

2. Mindful Consideration of Dietary Limits: When preparing the meal for your graduation celebration, consider dietary limitations and preferences. Include several diet-specific alternatives, such as vegetarian, vegan, gluten-free, and nut-free options. To assist customers in making educated decisions, clearly label the food products. If feasible, request dietary restrictions ahead of time to ensure that everyone has

excellent selections to choose from. Accepting varied dietary preferences demonstrates your concern for your visitors' well-being and ensures they may thoroughly enjoy the culinary pleasures.

3. enough Hydration Stations: Provide enough hydration stations throughout the party site to keep your guests refreshed and hydrated. Provide a variety of beverages, such as water, fruit-infused drinks, sodas, and non-alcoholic mocktails. Make these stations easily accessible and well-stocked so that guests may quench their thirst at any moment. Consider adding entertaining and decorative components to make the hydration stations more aesthetically appealing and welcoming.

4. Convenient Temperature Control: To guarantee your visitors' comfort, pay close attention to the temperature management of your party site. Adjust the heating and cooling systems according to the season. If you're throwing an outdoor party, give covered places, umbrellas, or cooling fans to keep attendees cool. Provide blankets or heaters to keep people warm if the weather is cool. A pleasant temperature helps people to

unwind and enjoy the festivities without disruptions.

5. Clean and conveniently accessible restrooms: Ensure your guests can access clean and easily accessible restrooms. Provide prominent signage or directions to the nearest facilities, and make sure they are well-stocked with necessities like toilet paper, soap, and hand sanitizers. Check and maintain the cleanliness of the bathrooms regularly throughout the party to create an excellent experience for your visitors.

6. Entertaining Entertainment for All Ages: Plan entertainment alternatives for guests of all ages and interests. Consider hiring a DJ or live band that can perform a variety of music genres to cater to a wide range of interests. Set up interactive activities, a picture booth, or a designated dance floor to engage attendees and promote involvement. Provide age-appropriate activities or a selected kids' zone to keep them occupied if children are present. Providing a varied choice of entertainment ensures that every attendee has a good time and creates a lively and welcoming party environment.

7. Thoughtful Special Needs Accommodations: Consider the needs of guests with impairments or special needs. Make sure your party location is wheelchair accessible, complete with ramps and accessible facilities. If necessary, provide reserved parking spaces or assistance to guests with mobility issues. Communicate with guests beforehand to learn about their requirements and make the appropriate arrangements to guarantee their comfort and enjoyment throughout the event.

8. Clear Communication and Directions: Make it simple for your guests to find their way to the party location by offering clear signs and directions—display signage for parking lots, entrances, bathrooms, and various activity zones. Use clear and concise communication to tell visitors about the timetable, key announcements, or any changes to the plan. Clear communication avoids uncertainty and allows visitors to participate fully in the celebration.

9. meaningful Gestures of Appreciation: Include expressive gestures of appreciation to thank your guests for joining you in this memorable event.

Make personalized thank-you cards, small party goodies, or commemorative tokens available for attendees to take home as a keepsake. Express your gratitude with a genuine speech or toast, honoring each individual's support and presence. These gestures create a warm and welcoming atmosphere and show your visitors how much you appreciate their facts.

10. Attentive Host or Hostess: As the host or hostess of the graduation celebration, your presence and attentiveness are critical in guaranteeing your guests' comfort and satisfaction. Greet each person politely, introduce them to others, and include them in talks. Circulate throughout the gathering, engaging with various groups and ensuring everyone has a lovely time. Attend to your guests' requirements, answer their inquiries, and resolve complaints immediately. You set the tone for a memorable and delightful visit by being an attentive and kind host.

Remember that a good graduation celebration is more than just décor and entertainment—it's about creating an atmosphere where your guests feel welcomed, at ease, and appreciated. You can guarantee that they have a fun and memorable time celebrating your accomplishments by considering their wants and preferences. When your visitors are at ease and interested, the party becomes a beautiful experience for everybody.

Addressing Possible Issues and Providing Troubleshooting Advice

While organizing a graduation celebration is an exciting activity, it is critical to be prepared for any obstacles that may occur along the road. From unexpected weather to logistical snags, proactively addressing these obstacles may help ensure a seamless and memorable celebration. You may overcome hurdles and create a unique graduation party experience by adopting a troubleshooting attitude and executing the following tips:

1. Mother Nature may be unpredictable, so having a backup plan for outdoor gatherings is crucial. If you're throwing an outdoor celebration, consider

renting a tent or marquee to give shelter in the event of rain or extreme heat. Prepare for unforeseen changes in weather by providing visitors with umbrellas or sunshades. Have an inside area ready to accommodate your gathering if the weather worsens.

2. Parking Issues: Inadequate parking can be a source of frustration for both hosts and guests. To address this issue, conduct prior research on local parking possibilities and offer straightforward advice to your guests on where to park. If parking is scarce, consider carpooling or shuttle services. If you're throwing a party in a residential neighborhood, be cautious of local restrictions and notify your neighbors beforehand to minimize difficulties.

3. Dietary Issues: It might be challenging to cater to different dietary restrictions and preferences, but with proper planning, it is feasible to accommodate everyone. To guarantee that your menu contains alternatives for vegetarians, vegans, gluten-free people, and those with food allergies, get dietary information from your visitors ahead of time. Communicate with your

caterer or prepare alternate foods to meet specific nutritional requirements. Label the food clearly so that guests may make educated decisions.

4. Technical Issues: If you include technology in your party, such as audio systems, projectors, or live streaming, technical issues may arise. Pre-test all equipment and have backup devices or specialists to troubleshoot any possible problems. Make a playlist or plan backup entertainment choices if your music system fails. Having a tech-savvy friend or family member on hand can help you quickly solve technical problems.

5. RSVP Problems: Dealing with RSVPs can be tricky since some visitors may need to remember to react or fail to answer on time. Set up a reminder system and send polite reminders a week before the celebration. Prepare for last-minute changes or cancellations and alter your plans appropriately. Extra food, beverages, and seating can assist in accommodating unexpected changes in the guest numbers.

6. Time Management: Graduation celebrations frequently have a set start and finish time, and

keeping the flow of events within that period is critical. Make a precise party schedule that includes the order of activities, speeches, and entertainment. Set out specified time windows for tasks to guarantee a smooth transition and minimize delays. Watch the clock and communicate with your MC or event organizer to stay on time.

7. Unexpected Guest Dynamics: With a mix of friends, relatives, and acquaintances in attendance, unexpected guest dynamics are always possible. Maintain a cheerful and inclusive environment in which everyone feels at ease. Encourage visitors to mingle by introducing them to one another, suggesting discussion topics, or organizing icebreaker games. Keep an eye on the party's energy and dynamics, and interfere gently if any disagreements or unpleasant situations occur.

8. Vendor Coordination: Effective communication and coordination are essential when working with outside suppliers like caterers, decorators, or entertainment. In advance, convey your goals, timetables, and particular requirements to the

providers. Establish a point of contact to supervise vendor setup and verify that the agreed-upon arrangements are followed. On the day of the celebration, check in with the vendors often to handle any difficulties as soon as possible.

9. Safety and Security: Your visitors' safety and security should always be top priorities. Consider any potential dangers in the party venue and take the appropriate procedures to reduce risks. Outdoor illumination should be adequate, and any steps or uneven terrain should be adequately marked. Encourage moderate drinking and give non-alcoholic alternatives if alcohol is served. Maintain a first-aid kit and appoint a responsible person to address any medical crises.

10. Adaptability and flexibility: Unforeseen obstacles might happen no matter how well you prepare. Throughout the party, it is critical to stay versatile and flexible. When confronted with unexpected events, be calm and attentive, and be ready to make rapid judgments or modifications as needed. Remember that the primary purpose of the celebration is to celebrate your graduation,

and your guests will appreciate your ability to manage any obstacles with grace.

You may overcome issues during your graduation celebration by anticipating them and having troubleshooting tools. Remember to be calm, think imaginatively, and seek help when necessary. A positive and proactive attitude can assist you in overcoming problems and ensuring that your guests have a flawless and delightful experience from beginning to end.

Chapter 8

Etiquette for Graduation Parties

Graduation parties are joyful gatherings of friends, family, and loved ones to commemorate an important milestone in someone's life. While the emphasis is on celebrating and having a good time, it's vital to remember that following some etiquette principles may assist in ensuring a seamless and pleasurable event for everyone. Here are a few pointers to help you navigate graduation party etiquette with elegance and courtesy:

1. Respond Responsibly: When you get an invitation to a graduation celebration, react quickly and clearly. Please let the host know whether or not you will be attending so they can plan appropriately. Indicate if you'll bring a visitor if there's a "plus one" option. This enables the

host to make food, seating, and other party-related preparations.

2. Timing is Everything: Arrive at the party on time or a little later than the scheduled start time. Arriving too early might place undue strain on the host, who may still be preparing while arriving too late can interrupt the event's flow. If you anticipate being late, please notify the host in advance so they can plan appropriately.

3. Express Gratitude: When you arrive at the party, meet and thank the host for inviting you. Thank them for their assistance in planning the occasion. A simple "thank you" goes a long way toward recognizing the host's efforts and hospitality.

4. Dress Appropriately: When determining what to wear, consider the dress code given on the invitation or the nature of the gathering. Graduation celebrations can range from casual backyard get-togethers to formal occasions. Dressing demonstrates regard for the event and the time and effort invested into preparing the meeting.

5. Mindful Mingling: Interact and interact with other visitors. Take advantage of the chance to network and congratulate the graduate. Attempt to involve people in your talks. Avoid taking up someone else's time and respect their personal space.

6. Be Aware of Dietary Restrictions: Please notify the host beforehand if you have any dietary restrictions or allergies. This enables them to satisfy your requirements or suggest alternatives if needed. Be respectful of others' dietary limitations while at the gathering. Avoid disparaging remarks about the meal or requesting extra accommodations that may interfere with the host's preparations.

7. Gift Giving: As a show of congratulations and support, it is traditional to provide a gift for the graduate. When choosing a present, consider the recipient's tastes and interests. It's a good idea to follow any gift registry instructions or suggestions supplied by the graduate. A thoughtful note or monetary present is always appreciated if you need help deciding what to give.

8. Respect the Space: Be respectful of the party location and your possessions. Unless specifically invited, avoid touching or disturbing decorations. If the party is being held at someone's house, respect their personal space and valuables. Clean up after yourself and dispose of waste correctly.

9. Participate in Activities: Participate in any planned activities or games. This demonstrates your excitement and contributes to a dynamic environment. Respect the host's efforts to organize entertainment and participate reasonably and inclusively with others.

10. Offer Assistance: If you sense the host or hostess might use some assistance, offer it. Serving food, cleaning up, or aiding with last-minute responsibilities shows your appreciation and eagerness to contribute to the celebration's success.

11. Follow-up Thank You: After attending the graduation celebration, sending a thank-you card or message to the host is customary. Express your appreciation for their hospitality, the pleasant time you had, and any particular highlights of the celebration that stood out for you.

By adhering to these graduation party etiquette recommendations, you can guarantee that you contribute positively to the celebration while honoring the host's efforts and creating a friendly environment for everyone participating. Graduation celebrations are supposed to be a time of pleasure and celebration, and following these etiquette guidelines can help make the event even more unique and memorable.

Proper Hostess Etiquette

Planning and organizing a graduation party entails many responsibilities on the host's side. It's not only about creating a party; it's also about making your visitors feel welcome, at ease, and appreciated. You may provide your visitors with an outstanding experience by following basic etiquette requirements. Here are some pointers on how to be a kind and attentive host:

1. Plan ahead of time: Begin arranging your graduation celebration early in advance to allow you adequate preparation time. Consider the

number of guests, the location, and the theme you wish to include. Planning ahead of time guarantees that you will be able to deal with any unforeseen obstacles and make the required plans.

2. Make a Guest List: Make a list of close family members, friends, and other loved ones who should attend this milestone event. Consider your venue's capacity and ensure you can adequately accommodate your guests. Include those who have had a significant impact on the graduate's life.

3. Send invites: Send out invites as soon as possible. Think about if you want to send paper invites or electronic invitations. Include all required information, such as the date, time, venue, and RSVP. Personalize the invites to match the subject or the graduate's personality if feasible.

4. Greet Your Visitors: As visitors arrive at the party, greet them warmly and sincerely. Take the time to appreciate and show your appreciation for their presence. Introduce visitors to one another,

especially if they are strangers, to encourage mixing and discussion.

5. Be a Good Host: It is critical for you, as the host, to be available to your guests during the celebration. Pay attention and engage in discussion so everyone feels included and at ease. Ensure your visitors have access to food, beverages, and other required facilities. Attend to their needs and handle any issues as soon as possible.

6. Provide Food and Drinks: Create a menu based on the theme and tastes of your visitors. When choosing meals, keep dietary limitations and allergies in mind. To accommodate varied preferences, provide a choice of foods and beverages. Arrange the food in an orderly and appealing manner, making it readily available to guests.

7. Entertainment and Activities: Plan activities and entertainment to keep your guests involved and amused. Provide alternatives for diverse age groups and interests, whether live music, games, or a picture booth. Ascertain that the

entertainment complements the overall concept and mood of the gathering.

8. Consider your guests' comfort: Consider your guests' comfort during the gathering. Provide plenty of sitting, shade, or warmth depending on the weather and site. Consider the flow of the party and organize the area so that people can walk around freely and chat comfortably.

9. Express Appreciation: Thank your guests for attending the graduation party. Please take a minute to thank them individually for their presence and for sharing this momentous occasion with you and the graduate. Handwritten thank-you letters or personalized mementos of appreciation can be a great way to express your thanks.

10. Be Mindful of Your Neighbors: If you're throwing a party at your house or in a residential neighborhood, be mindful of your neighbors. Inform them about the party and any potential noise or parking arrangements beforehand. To avoid any disruption, avoid making excessive noise late at night and make sure your visitors park appropriately.

11. Follow-Up Communication: Send your visitors a follow-up letter or thank-you note after the celebration. Thank you again, and please share any highlights or memorable moments from the party. This gesture shows your appreciation for their presence and contributes to strengthening your connections.

As a host, you create a friendly and comfortable environment for your visitors by following the correct etiquette. Your effort and attention to detail will be appreciated, ensuring everyone has a memorable graduation party. Remember that your goal as the host is to encourage relationships, create a joyous atmosphere, and ensure that everyone departs with fond recollections of this momentous day.

Guidelines for Gift-Giving

Giving a nice gift during a graduation celebration is a lovely way to honor the graduate's accomplishments and show your support. However, navigating the world of gift-giving may be difficult at times. Here are some recommendations to follow to ensure your present is well-received and meaningful:

1. Consider the Graduate's Interests: When choosing a present, consider the graduate's interests, hobbies, and future goals. Consider what they are enthusiastic about or may require when they begin their new chapter in life. Personalizing the present to suit their personality and goals provides a personal touch.

2. Practicality and Usability: Select a practical and beneficial presentation to the graduate. Consider office supplies, digital devices, or professional clothes as gifts to help them in their future efforts. Practical presents demonstrate that you have considered their needs and supported their journey after graduation.

3. Symbolic and Sentimental presents: Symbolic or sentimental gifts may profoundly impact the graduate. It may be jewelry, a customized item, or anything representing a shared experience or an inside joke. These presents elicit emotions and generate lasting memories for the graduate,

reminding them of this crucial milestone in their lives.

4. Gift Cards and Monetary presents: If you are unaware of the graduate's preferences or needs, gift cards or monetary presents might be a good option. They enable the graduate to pick something meaningful or commit cash to critical conditions. Consider giving them a gift card to a company or restaurant that caters to their interests.

5. collective Gifting: Consider collaborating with friends or family to present a joint gift. This allows for a more significant skill or experience that the graduate will remember. Coordination with others is required to ensure the present is coherent and well-coordinated, reflecting the graduate's collaborative support and joy.

6. Handmade or DIY presents: Handmade or DIY gifts can be extremely meaningful and one-of-a-kind. Consider using your abilities and expertise to make something special for the graduate. These presents, whether a scrapbook of memories, unique artwork, or a handwritten note, demonstrate your thinking and effort.

7. Cash Gift Etiquette: Consider doing it tastefully and courteously if you make a monetary gift. A handwritten message of congratulations and best wishes might be included with the cash or cheque. It is considered rude to mention the actual amount of the present.

8. Presentation and Wrapping: Make an effort to display and package your gift. A present that is nicely wrapped gives a sense of excitement and expectation. Pay attention to details such as a handwritten message or a colorful ribbon to improve the overall appearance. Your thoughtfulness is reflected in your care and attention to the packaging.

9. Be careful of Cultural or Religious issues: When choosing a present, be cautious of cultural or religious matters. Some cultures may have unique gift-giving practices or traditions. To ensure your gift is suitable and courteous, study and understand cultural sensitivities.

10. Obey the host's wishes: If the host has provided any gift preferences or requests, follow through on them. They can recommend a specific gift registry or prefer charitable donations over

traditional gifts. Respect their choices and select a present accordingly.

Remember that the thinking and sentiment behind the present are the most significant aspects of it. The gesture is more important than the monetary value. The gift should express your joy in the graduate and your best wishes for their future success.

Finally, Congrats and Best Wishes

As we conclude this e-book journey, we'd like to extend our final congratulations and best wishes to the graduate. You have attained a significant life milestone, and your perseverance, persistence, and devotion have paid off. Take a minute to think about what you've done and the exciting adventure ahead.

Graduation is more than a finish line; it is a stepping stone to a world of possibilities. As you progress, accept the obstacles, grasp the chances, and pursue your ambitions with unshakable zeal.

Remember that you are capable of great things, and your graduation party is an opportunity to celebrate the magnificent person you have become.

Surround yourself with people who raise you and encourage you. Your family, friends, and mentors have been at your side every step of the way, offering advice, support, and love. Thank them and let them know how much their assistance has meant to you. Take advantage of this opportunity to rejoice together and make memories that will last a lifetime.

Remember the lessons you've learned, the connections you've formed, and the events that have influenced you as you begin this new chapter. Your education has provided you with the information, skills, and capacity to change the world positively. Use your skills to inspire, motivate, and positively contribute to your community and beyond.

Remember that success is measured not just by your achievements or financial wealth but also by your influence on others and the joy you find in following your dreams. Follow your heart, pursue your aspirations, and enjoy the ride with an open mind and an unwavering spirit. The route may be winding, but each stride will bring you closer to a destiny entirely yours.

We want to express our deepest congratulations and best wishes to you, the graduate. May your graduation party be a celebration of your accomplishments and a springboard to a bright future. May it be a joyous occasion full of laughter and silent moments. May the memories made on this memorable occasion constantly remind you of your strength and the limitless opportunities that await you.

Finally, we remind you that you are capable, talented, and destined for greatness. Believe in yourself, enjoy the adventure, and never lose sight of your incredible potential. Congratulations on attaining this significant milestone once more. May your graduation celebration be the ideal kickoff to an astonishing adventure. Cheers to a prosperous, joyful, and fulfilling future!

Congratulations, and may your journey be blessed with limitless opportunities and tremendous accomplishments!

Conclusion

Congratulations! You've arrived after your e-book adventure, having explored a wide range of graduation party ideas and gaining vital insights about how to design a grand celebration. Reflecting on the information presented, it is evident that a graduation party is more than simply a gathering—it is an occasion to recognize accomplishments, make lasting memories, and celebrate the exciting move into a new chapter of life.

We've covered everything from choosing themes that set the tone for an outstanding event to managing logistics, entertaining attendees, and navigating correct etiquette throughout this e-book. We've looked at imaginative ideas, practical advice, and genuine gestures that might help make your graduation celebration a smashing success.

Remember that the goal of a graduation party is more than just entertainment. It is an opportunity to recognize the graduate's hard work, commitment, and advancement. It is time to show thanks for the help of family, friends, and mentors who have been instrumental in this journey. It celebrates accomplishments and is a launching pad toward an unknown future.

Keep the significance of personalization in mind as you design your graduation celebration. Customize the event to suit the graduate's personality and interests. Customize the possibility to do the graduate's personality and interests. Infuse the party with components that resonate with their passions and objectives, whether through theme, décor, meal, or entertainment. This ensures that the celebration is not only entertaining but also genuinely meaningful.

Also, believe in the power of your imagination. Allow your creativity to go wild as you experiment with new ideas and put your touch on old favorites. Let your creativity show through every facet of the event, from DIY décor and personalized party favors to imaginative themes and engaging activities. Your efforts will be recognized, and your guests will be intrigued by the care and uniqueness of your event.

Remember the significance of structure and attention to detail as you go through the planning process. Make a detailed timetable, a budget, and all necessary arrangements well in advance. This will assist to reduce tension and ensure that the event runs smoothly and smoothly. Remember that preparation is the key to success, and a well-organized party allows you to enjoy the festivities with your guests thoroughly.

Finally, always emphasize your guests' comfort and happiness. Consider their requirements, preferences, and any special accommodations that may be necessary. Your visitors will feel liked and valued by creating a welcoming environment, providing good entertainment, and ensuring everyone is adequately cared for. Their presence brings vitality and enthusiasm to the festivities, and their happiness should be prioritized.

Finally, a graduation party is an exceptional occasion to recognize accomplishments, create lifetime memories, and express thanks. It is a moment to honor the graduate and the support system that has helped them along the way. Make your celebration remarkable for everybody involved by infusing it with creativity, individuality, and meaningful gestures.

So go ahead and start celebrating! Use the ideas, recommendations, and guidelines in this e-book to design a graduation celebration that will leave you and your guests speechless. Cherish the moments, appreciate the accomplishments, and look forward to the next chapter of your life with excitement and delight. Congratulations once more, and best wishes for a fantastic graduation party!